Praise for *The Tao of Motivation*

'Few investments are risk free. Motivation is one of them. This practical and engaging guide helps to show you the way.'
Adair Turner - Director-General, Confederation of British Industries

'This book is a rich and vivid mix of serious theory, witty practice and handy models. It left me full of ideas, prompted to swing into action, and of course . . . thoroughly motivated.'
Rita Clifton - Chief Executive, Interbrand

'In a world of tight deadlines and heavy pressure, motivating people is more important than ever. *The Tao of Motivation* provides a wealth of practical tips, relevant stories and a good dose of humour.'
Carolyn Fairbairn - Director of Strategy, BBC Worldwide

'The wise invest in motivating people. This book shows you how.'
Charles Alexander - Managing Director, Lehman Brothers

'Interested in motivation? Then read this book - you're worth it. Not interested in motivation? Then buy a book on preparing your cv instead.'
Patrick Dunne - Director, 3i plc

'Successful leaders inspire ordinary people to achieve the extraordinary. This book is motivational. It will help you get the best out of your colleagues and yourself.'
Christopher Rodrigues - Group Chief Executive, Bradford & Bingley Building Society

'The skill of motivation is neither a charisma contest, nor an impenetrable science. This book provides refreshingly practical insights, and is an engaging read.'
Roger Holmes - Managing Director, Woolworths plc

'At the heart of leadership is the ability to motivate - whether it comes naturally or not. This book is a must-read.'
Ruth Tait - Head of PA Executive Search and Selection

Also by Max Landsberg

*The Tao of Coaching – Boost Your
Effectiveness at Work by Inspiring and
Developing Those Around You*

THE TAO OF MOTIVATION

INSPIRE YOURSELF AND OTHERS

Max Landsberg

HarperCollinsBusiness
An Imprint of HarperCollins*Publishers*

HarperCollins*Publishers*
77 - 85 Fulham Palace Road,
Hammersmith, London W6 8JB

Published by HarperCollins*Publishers* 1999
1 3 5 7 9 10 8 6 4 2

A catalogue record for this book
is available from the British Library

ISBN 0 00 257031 9

Set in Garamond by
Rowland Phototypesetting Ltd, Bury St Edmunds, Suffolk

Printed and bound in Great Britain by
Caledonian International Book Manufacturing Ltd, Glasgow

To the memory of my grandparents
Ann and William, Max and Hedwig

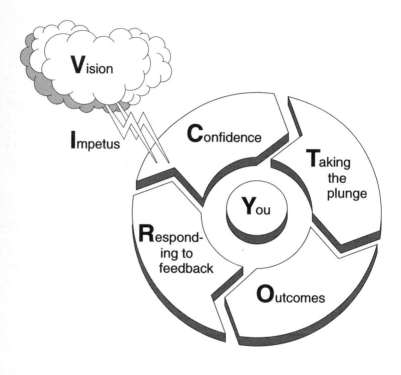

For the movements of a man's life are in spirals:
we go back whence we came,
ever returning on our former traces,
only upon a higher level,
on the next upward coil of the spiral,
so that it is a going backward and a going forward
ever and both at once.

George MacDonald (1824 – 1905),
England's Antiphon

Contents

INTRODUCTION

You *have* it. It's in your hands. You have the key
to motivating other people and yourself.

What is the most important thing in the world? Money, power, sex?
Food, shelter, security? Love? Health?

Vital though these things are, there is something equally essential – the
ability to motivate yourself and other people. For with the skill and
habit of motivation come the ability to breathe life into your dreams,
or perhaps even to dare to dream in the first place!

*Motivation. The skill of energising yourself (or someone else) to
accomplish something amazing. Involves a series of steps: creating a
vision and impetus, cultivating confidence, taking the plunge,
observing outcomes and overcoming obstacles, responding constructively to feedback. These steps reinforce each other, primarily
through building confidence.*

The skill of self-motivation is what propels the successful person to
achieve still more, impels the down-trodden as they raise themselves
by their own bootstraps, and fosters the growth of us all.

Of course, if you can help someone else to become more motivated,
then you will have given them an unforgettable gift. Not surprisingly,
you cannot nowadays be a leader in business unless you are a motivator of your people.

But the importance of this skill extends well beyond the workplace.
For we are all sometime leaders of something – of a family, a group of
friends, a sports team, a friend in need.

Furthermore, in a world which is becoming ever less predictable, there
is perhaps only one source of true security – knowing that you can

motivate yourself, whatever the circumstances which might intrude upon you.

Two further points:

1. **You can't motivate someone else if you are not motivated yourself; and the converse is usually true.** That is one reason why this book is entitled *The Tao of Motivation*. Taoism holds that things (even apparent opposites) are intimately connected with each other. The familiar yin-yang symbol symbolises this point. Were you ever motivated by someone who – themselves – was not motivated? Do you not yourself feel motivated when you have helped someone else to achieve this state?

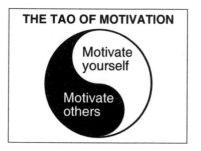

2. **Waste no time on the semantic question of whether feeling 'motivated in general' is different from feeling 'motivated to accomplish a specific goal'.** Most people, if motivated in a few specific areas of their lives, will feel generally motivated. Any distinction is artificial.

What you can expect from this book

By the time you've read this book, and applied some of its suggestions, you should be able to motivate yourself to accomplish a specific goal, become more 'motivated' in general and have a surprisingly similar effect on other people.

Amazingly, the skill of motivation is rarely taught, save by the slings, arrows and lucky happenstance of our lives. This book aims to fill that gap by providing a few simple tools and techniques which have worked for many people over many years.

Nevertheless, any book is only a guide. Practice makes perfect and I have taken the liberty of suggesting some exercises: simple ways to 'take the plunge' in developing your motivational skills in interaction with other people.

Structure of the book

The first half of this book explains a simple but powerful technique for motivating yourself and others. The second half of the book explains the related essentials of practical psychology - the minimum amount you need to function as a manager; points which I am sure you will find relevant beyond the workplace.

* * *

In summary: the motivational person seeks not just for themselves or someone else to feel better, but also for him or her to see the reinvigorating rewards of redoubled efforts.

In today's world of business (at least), consistent high energy and focus are essential for personal success and happiness. I hope that this book will help you and others towards a rapid addiction to the positive habit of motivation.

Max Landsberg
London, 1999

Napoleon has a bad hair day . . .

**To lead others, you need to
motivate them; to motivate
people, you need first to
motivate yourself**

1. Motivation and the Three Dimensions of Leadership

In which Alex faces the dawning realisation that he needs to spread some inspiration

Alex had returned from vacation. Although his suitcase was light, like his wallet, his shoulders nevertheless drooped slightly. For a week he had waited for the phone call. The one which would congratulate him on his election to the Board of Directors.

But that call had never come. Although the Chairman had called him for a brief conversation, he had not revealed anything definite. And now Alex feared that no news would turn out to be *bad* news.

Taking his suntan as protection, he ventured to his executive office on the tenth floor of the company's global headquarters. As he greeted his secretary Julia cheerily, he wondered what she knew about his career prospects. She gave nothing away. '. . . Oh yes,' she finished nonchalantly, 'by the way, Jim wants to see you at 9.30.'

Jim was a very direct chap. He was also Alex's boss. Alex knew that the outstretched hand of welcome would simultaneously be signalling a thumbs-up or a thumbs-down. Alex wondered which it would be.

He was saved from further speculation as Jim arrived unexpectedly. 'Good vacation?' asked Jim. Alex knew that the question was merely rhetorical as Jim sat down opposite him and continued, 'Sorry I couldn't call you. Bit difficult, you see. Best not to beat about the bush. I'm afraid we couldn't get you appointed to the Board . . .'

Alex's head swam. This had been his last chance, and everyone knew it. Alex tried to pay attention, but his mind lurched erratically between fast-forward and reverse gear. 'What will I tell Sarah?' 'What was the name of that bar in Greece, in which we were sitting only last week?' 'Is Jim going to fire me?' Several hours later, Alex would arrive at the following artist's reconstruction of the killer speech.

'You see, Alex, we all think that you're great at what you do. You've identified attractive acquisition candidates for the company, led some major reorganisations and made important contributions during meetings of the Executive Committee.

'But we're in a business where people really matter. These people need to be *motivated and inspired*, not just managed. While your teams do see you as a coach, there is a feeling that you are just going through the motions of coaching. Perhaps not paying enough attention to truly inspirational leadership. I'm afraid the company is getting tougher on this aspect of leadership – especially when it comes to electing Directors.'

Alex's adrenalin eventually kicked in and he heard, in real time, Jim's final comments, 'I know you'll need some time to absorb all this. There's a role we need to fill – in charge of Special Projects. We think you should move down there for a month or two. It'll help you to think things over.'

'Are you saying that I have no future with the company?' mumbled Alex. Then, with more resolve, 'That can't be right!'

'Look, Alex, real leaders have three things in common: the intelligence and artistry to develop an exciting vision of where the team should be heading; the enthusiasm to inspire the team, customers and other people with that vision; and the self-motivation, charisma and problem-solving skills to keep the team and individuals energised and on course. It all adds up to the ability to motivate other people.

'We're not saying that you necessarily lack these skills. It's just that we haven't seen them in sufficient quantity. So you're not being fired. But you should take some time to think about whether you are able – and keen – to demonstrate these skills. I could quite understand it if you said, "To hell with the company" and decided to move on. I certainly can't promise you a promotion in the near future.'

Alex knew precisely what this meant. Special Projects were never very special. That department was a temporary parking place for senior executives who were on their way out. 'Thinking things over' meant finding another company to work for. Alex knew he was moving to Death Row. There would be little chance of a pardon. And his only companions would be the Faded Five – a handful of junior staff whom the company could not employ in more meaningful roles.

* * *

Alex sat motionless for a few minutes after Jim's departure from his office. Then he headed out of the building for a walk, to clear his thinking. Emerging from the lift, he squinted into the sunlight which flooded through the revolving doors and across the reception area. As if propelled by sunbeams, a figure approached him. It was Michael, the former Chief Financial Officer of the company and once a mentor to Alex. Michael now served as a non-executive Director of the company for a few days a month. 'Alex, how are you? Haven't seen you for a while. Just back from vacation?'

'Yes . . . but I've just had an unpleasant surprise.'

Michael suspected that Alex now knew of the Board's decision, but checked anyway, 'Just met with Jim?'

'Yes . . . look, any chance that we could get together later today?'

Michael hesitated, '. . . I've got meetings all day, Alex.' But he knew that Alex needed some support, 'We could have a quick drink at around 6.30, if you'd like to.'

Alex jumped at the chance. He knew he'd have to tell Sarah the grim news when he arrived home. Perhaps a prior talk with Michael would help him to rehearse his lines. And maybe Michael could help in a more substantial way, too . . .

Motivation and Leadership

There are many reasons for developing the skill and habit of motivation. Perhaps the primary reasons are: a) to become a more effective leader, and b), more generally, to be a positive, philanthropic force in the world.

We can each choose whether to be philanthropic. But succeeders in business tend to be leaders, and, outside the workplace, the need to lead is often thrust upon us – whether or not we consciously seek it. Most of us are sometime leaders of *something*: a company, a working team, a sports team, a family, a group of friends on an outing to see a film; at the very least we lead *ourselves*.

Much has been written on leadership, but it all seems to boil down to a single formula, explained on the facing page:

Leadership = Vision x Inspiration x Momentum

Note that, although the leader focuses initially on developing a Vision, and then on Inspiration and Momentum in turn, he or she also continues to work along all these dimensions, as the mission progresses. In addition, leaders each have their own style, but true leaders pass a minimum threshold on *all three* dimensions. The Visionary who cannot inspire is not a leader. Nor is the Momentum-sustainer who lacks Vision.

* * *

But our subject is *motivation*, so what is the relationship between it and leadership?

- It's unlikely that you can be an effective leader if you can't motivate other people.

- Motivation is closely entwined *with all three* dimensions of leadership.

- While all leaders need to motivate, not all motivators need to be leaders. You can apply the skills of motivation 'just' to help a friend.

The remainder of this book aims to provide you with a few memorable and practical tools to help you motivate yourself and other people. Chapter 2 presents the first of these tools. But first complete the checklist in Appendix B, page 123, to help you focus your development.

The Three Dimensions of Leadership

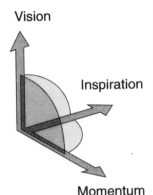

Vision

Inspiration

Momentum

Vision: being smart enough to decide what needs to be done (a radically new idea, or an old idea whose time is now ripe), and artistic enough to paint compelling images of both the destination and the nature of the journey.

Inspiration: being a good enough salesperson to enroll others to the vision, the journey, and the team.

Momentum: having enough self-motivation, charisma, people skills and problem-solving abilities to keep the team and individuals energised and on course.

Illustrations of Leadership

	Work	*Family*	*Self*
1. Vision	'Buy up regional radio licences, and create a national network'	'The family vacation of a lifetime'	'Returning to being a non-smoker'
2. Inspiration	Enrol interested parties; build team	Appeal to family members' individual enthusiasms	Engage all parts of the self (beyond just concerns for health, savings, etc.)
3. Momentum	Monitor progress; overcome obstacles; keep team or personal spirit 'up'		

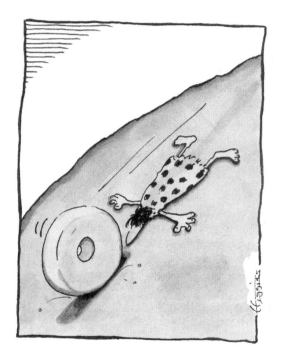

Oonga becomes the first victim of a vicious circle.

Create a virtuous cycle of *vision, confidence, effort, results* and reinforcing *responses to feedback*

2. VICTORY – the Essence of Motivation

In which Alex discovers a simple diagram which will change his life for ever

Later in the evening, in the pub which lay a stone's throw from the office, Alex attacked the bar, 'Two whiskies, please. Doubles.'

Michael had helped Alex on many occasions in the past five years, so Alex trusted him and felt able to recount Jim's comments directly, as they settled into a quiet corner, '. . . so the company sees me as a good administrator and manager – and even with an ability to coach – but it doesn't see me as an inspirer, a motivator, and a leader'.

'And how does that make you feel?' probed Michael.

'Lousy,' replied Alex. 'They just don't know how good I really am. I'm great at motivating people. Just ask any of my teams.'

'We did.' The eyes of the unfortunate listener widened. 'Alex, I'm afraid you can't avoid this one. You'll need to address it head on. And you need to tackle this motivation thing not just for work, but for other aspects of your life, too. We've talked in the past about your management style – logic and control, albeit coupled with insight and intuition. But I think you're ready to work on the skills needed to *motivate* and *inspire* people. Perhaps I'm out of line here, but I think your family would see the benefits, too.

'Now that I've retired I have a more relaxed schedule. I'd be happy to help you. I'm not sure if it will be in time to help you progress in the company. But, either way, your life must go on and I'm sure that working on your ability to get people fired up will be really worthwhile.'

Alex wasn't sure he was enjoying this discussion. All he wanted was someone with whom to share his sorrows, but now he was on the receiving end of something that sounded like a lecture. 'How do you think you might help me, Michael?' he asked half-heartedly.

Michael asked Alex what he'd concluded so far, regarding his current predicament. Alex replied that, during the course of the afternoon, he had visited the Special Projects department. He had met with the Faded Five and seen that the current Special Project was to review all the customer complaints of the last year. This was a pet hobby of the Chairman, but no-one else really seemed interested – including the five team members.

He also told Michael that he'd been trying to decide how to spend the next few months. He'd either focus on searching for another job, or he'd prove the company wrong by doing a great piece of work on the Special Project. But he couldn't decide which to focus on.

'What's all this "either/or" thinking, Alex? You know perfectly well that motivating the Faded Five would be more about *how* you interacted with them and far less about the total amount of time you invested in the team. Why not do both: aim to do an outstanding job on the project *and also* create a safety net by finding a possible position outside the company? That way, if you do end up leaving, you won't feel as if you've been a failure.'

Alex had difficulty in listening to the criticism. But it was clear that Michael really believed in him. That made the feedback more palatable – and even a bit inspiring. Eventually he asked Michael for a few tips in case he decided to opt for motivating the team.

'OK, Alex. I have to leave shortly, but I'll give you all I know about motivation in a few summary points. I'll also give you a diagram which someone explained to me fifteen years ago and which has always worked whenever I've used it.'

As Alex grew intrigued, Michael continued, 'Most of these points are as relevant to motivating yourself as they are to motivating other people – but I'm sure you'll be able to figure out the overlaps for yourself.

'Point one, **to motivate someone else you need *genuinely* to be motivated yourself**. This sounds obvious, but it's amazing how many managers and leaders are motivated without conveying their excitement – or are uninspired while pretending to be motivated. People spot pretence easily. If you can't get motivated about your current role, then change to a role which does excite you, and where your excitement will motivate others.

'Point two, **focus on motivating the other person in a *specific* area of their work or life**. Some people try to make a distinction between "feeling more motivated in general" and "being motivated to accomplish some specific goal". Don't waste time with that conundrum. Take it from me: if someone is motivated in a few specific areas of their life, they'll soon start to feel motivated about life in general.

'Point three, **be an *artist*, not a lecturer**. Much of motivation is about getting someone to engage with an image of success. You have to use your artistic skills to conjure up a really compelling picture of what that person, or team, might achieve. And of course, each artist needs to know his or her audience – the vision you develop for someone needs to engage their personality.

'Point four: **en-courage**. Interesting word. Give them courage. To do this, praise often helps! In this era of 999 degree feedback, people at work are bombarded continually with messages that are mixed: positive statements almost always being accompanied by implied criticism. So deliver some unadulterated praise – *whenever* it's warranted. Other tips: help them to see their progress, and how their progress fits into the wider vision (the vision for themselves, for the team, or for the company). Help them to check that they are not subconsciously demotivating themselves through unhealthy self-talk.

'Finally, you need to pace yourself for a **marathon, not a sprint**. It's unlikely that you'll motivate someone in an instant. Pace your support – in terms of time, patience and praise – to last the course. Naturally, this all applies to motivating yourself as well as to motivating other people.'

Michael finished his drink, as Alex reflected. 'That's helpful as a background, but how do you motivate someone to accomplish something *specific*?'

Michael reached for his pocket, took out a pen, and flipped two beer mats so they were blank-side up. 'This is where the diagram comes in. We'll have to talk about the details some other time, but let me just sketch it out for you. It's called the **VICTORY** cycle. I guarantee, it has a 100 per cent success rate . . .'*

---

*The points from the beer mats are included on the next two pages.

The VICTORY Loop of Motivation

Motivating yourself or someone else involves a series of steps: motivation is a *process*, rarely a one-off act.

It is also a process which is *iterative*: the steps need to be reinforced as you retread the circle a few times.

The five steps are as follows:

- **Vision.** Perhaps the most critical step is to develop a compelling vision of 'success'. You can rarely develop this picture in a vacuum – it needs to grow from some reality: your image of a person whom you admire or loathe(!), through conversations with others, or through inspired 'imagination'. Also, a vision is rarely 'intellectual'. Visions are most useful when they engage all six senses, and when they provide the basis for a simple plan of action. See Chapter 3 on Vision and Chapter 16 on NLP.

- **Confidence.** 'Con-fidence' comes from the Latin meaning 'with faith'. A vision strongly held will build faith and confidence. Chapter 5 illustrates other ways to build confidence. Chapter 17 addresses praise.

- **Taking the plunge.** Eventually you have to take some sort of action towards your goal. Sometimes this requires 'diving in at the deep end'. But if you have filled the pool, so to speak (with a substantial vision), and you have the confidence of knowing that you can swim, you will survive and perhaps excel (Chapter 6).

- **Outcomes and obstacles.** Your efforts will be repaid, with or without the help of luck (Chapter 7).

- **Responding to feedback.** Your outlook and – in turn – your confidence will be determined as much by how you *respond* to the feedback from yourself and others as by the actual outcomes or feedback themselves (Chapter 8 for Responding to Feedback).

Of course, the Y of VICTORY stands for You – as characterised by the underlying factors which motivate you (Chapter 9) and your successes.

As a high-level summary, this is the essence of motivating yourself – and of motivating others.

The Virtuous Circle

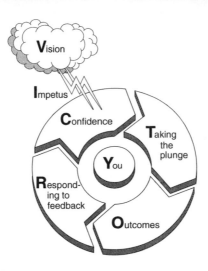

✓ With an energising vision and impetus: confidence is strong, efforts are redoubled, results impressive, feedback uplifting, and confidence reinforced. You will be motivated.

✖ Without a vision and impetus: efforts are hesitant, results mediocre, responses disappointing, and confidence diminished; you will feel demotivated.

Exercise

1. As a reminder, jot the above model in your diary – or onto a sticker – *now*.

2. Find an opportunity to test this model on yourself or others.

   • Does it help you understand your positive or negative feelings about a current challenge?

   • Which parts of the cycle can you affect most rapidly?

Somehow, the new school of abstraction left Ted unmoved.

A powerful vision creates confidence and catalyses action

3. Vision

In which Alex finds that his ability to develop a vision depends on a little practice, not on his genes

Neither New Age man nor international footballer, Alex refused to shed tears as he broke to his wife the bad news that he had not been appointed a Director of the company. Later that evening she helped Alex to see the merits of the 'both, and' path for the next few months – rather than the 'either, or' strategy. He would *both* look for another job *and* develop his skills in motivating others.

Returning to work the next morning, he didn't exactly have a *vision* for himself, but he at least felt committed to a clear objective. In three months' time – by Christmas – he would have accomplished three things. He would have successfully completed the Special Project, turned the Faded Five into an elite team and found an exciting job outside the company. Challenging objectives. But, having decided some goals which were concrete, he at least felt a bit energised.

That morning, he took stock of the customer complaints project. Thousands of complaints, about hundreds of products, sat politely and silently in the computer. No picture yet of where the main problems were. And then there were the Faded Five . . . Rob, Bill, Emma, Jerry and Kate. He'd get to know them better during the next few months, but his initial fifteen-minute chat with each of them did not fill him with confidence about either their skill or their will.

'OK,' he said to himself, 'let's get this project organised.' As normal in these situations, he started by preparing a detailed plan, which took account of all the relationships between the sub-tasks.

'Oh no! There I go again – all plans and no big picture; no vision.' He shoved aside the plans. Grabbing a blank sheet of paper, he started his search for a vision for the project. For ten minutes, he jotted down words, phrases and images as they came to him ... 'using customer complaints to advantage ... swords into ploughshares ... the sword Excalibur ... customer not as enemy but as ally ... landing on the beaches ... Churchill ...' He was *scared*. He'd never done this before. He was worried that he might have discovered an exciting and powerful technique which he should have been using for the last twenty-five years! Of course, this technique was so wacky that he could never admit to using it. But he carried on for the full ten minutes.

Then he reviewed his three sheets of scribbles. He circled a few ideas that seemed to have the greatest potential. 'Alchemy – yes, turning base metal into gold, or customer complaints into initiatives of value. Sounds too mystical though. Not enough *action*, not enough about customer-as-partner.' At last he settled on *Excalibur* as the theme for the project – he remembered the excitement with which his nephew Jack had listened to the stories of King Arthur the night before.

'So, what do I do with this?' his quizzical expression turned gradually to a smile. 'Of course ... our project and team has no identity yet. We need a name ... Project Excalibur. We will be a team of King Arthurs who pull the sword of competitive advantage out of the opaque stone of customer complaints.'

He spent another ten minutes playing with the metaphor. It seemed to be working. But what about the mission's main steps? The theme was engaging, but how could he weave in a few action steps when he shared his vision with the team? He started at the end: they would extract the metaphorical sword by Christmas Eve, three months away.

Now, how about the intermediate steps? All that data in the computer: they needed some magical formula for converting the data into something useful. Rob knew something about computer programming. Yes! – he would be Merlin the Magician ... Ten minutes later Alex had drafted a vision and a plan, and some possible roles for all five of the team members.

Alex sat back and reflected. 'This looks nothing like the way I would normally start a project. Images instead of complexities. But it's made *me* excited. Let's just hope it works with the team.'

He hesitated before convening the team. Perhaps he should be using the football metaphor which his earlier brainstorming had generated? But Excalibur – with all its rich associated imagery – had become imprinted in his mind indelibly. He paused only to jot one word in his diary: Alchemist. This would be his vision for *himself* over the next three months. He would transform the team into a motivated squad and he would transform himself into a motivator of others.

*   *   *

Alex gathered the team. He unveiled his vision, communicating it with a genuine passion and conviction that surprised both him and the team. At first uncertain, they became convinced as Alex fleshed out the project's milestones and the team's roles. They even started to contribute ideas, which Alex tried to incorporate.

The meeting lasted forty-five minutes. In some sense they had accomplished nothing. They had not generated detailed plans; they had not allocated responsibilities with military precision. But that was the *old* way of reckoning. They had, in fact, accomplished much: they had a clear, engaging and energising vision of where they were heading, knew the main rivers to be crossed, mountains to be climbed and roles which each team member would be playing. These things would serve the team well in the course of the project. They had also generated some early action steps – thus inspiring each other with enthusiasm and building some initial momentum for the project.

*   *   *

During the next few days Alex spent time with Rob, Bill, Emma, Jerry and Kate. He worked with them on their individual plans for accomplishing their parts of the project. He also revisited occasionally the vision for the project, and the vision for each team member's role.

Rob, for example, had been very anxious. The company had never made much use of his computer skills and Rob had felt that his days were numbered. Alex tried logic: Rob might as well spend the next three months building and honing his skill in using databases. This he could then apply within the company, or use on his job applications to other firms. But without overdoing it, Alex used vision to complement logic. It was Rob's self-image as a Merlin – acquiring magical powers that he could take to distant lands – which really picked his spirits up.

Developing and Sharing a Vision

Developing a compelling and vital Vision of the destination, and of the major steps of the journey, is the first step in the VICTORY cycle. It is the prerequisite for any sustained motivation – of yourself, or of other people. You will return periodically to this Vision, as you take further steps on the VICTORY cycle. Without a strong Vision, there is a risk of becoming lost in the psychic smog of personal insecurity.

In developing the Vision:

- Use your *imagination* – you are, after all, creating an *image*.

- Engage all your senses in developing and expressing your image. How many senses do you have? Well, there are the familiar five senses, then there's the sixth sense, then add the sense of humour, sense of balance (or vertigo), sense of duty . . . employ them all.

- Test, however, that your Vision is useful. The acid test is whether you can use it, or some part of it, to create a *very simple (one-page) plan of action* to get you going. This plan triggers the lightning-stroke link between the Vision and the other parts of the VICTORY cycle. Don't become bogged down in planning – just jot down some important steps.

If you are motivating someone else, or a team of people, you will clearly need to share your Vision. In doing so:

- *Bring your Vision to life by any means possible.* Using words alone may not be enough. In some cases, where the goal is to develop a specific skill, the most powerful route may be by demonstration. (This will prove the achievability of the goal.)

- *Involve the other person/people in developing the Vision further.* The resulting Vision will be far more memorable.

- Nevertheless, *present your initial draft of the Vision forcefully* – for by merely 'daring the team to be great', you are taking the first step in building its confidence.

- Finally, remember to *re-express the Vision periodically*, as you take yourself or others through the VICTORY cycle.

Vision

The Vision should:

- Be a compelling image of the destination, and the major steps of the journey

- Engage as many senses as possible

- Stimulate a simple plan of action, to energise the rest of the VICTORY cycle

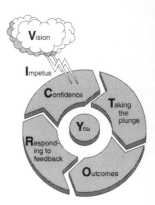

Examples of good and poor visions

✖	✔	Comment
Become pre-eminent in space exploration	Land a man on the moon, by the end of the decade	Specific, not vague
End racism	'I have a dream . . .'	A true vision, with indelible impact
Let's be patriotic	'God for Harry, England, and St George'	Engages personally, appealing to piety and duty
Beware of radioactive hazard	☢	Engages visually

Exercise

- Complete Appendix C (page 124).

The Sisters of Saint Anne seriously consider rejecting 'piety' as their primary motivation, in favour of something a little more exciting.

Harness visceral urges to transform yourself positively

4. Impetus – money, power, sex, respect, jealousy, pride, duty, perfection, hope . . .

In which Alex meets his makers

Alex now felt slightly happier. He had started to engage the members of his team in a common vision, though he knew he would need to do more if they were to commit to that vision in earnest. However, he thought he should be making more progress on his search for a job.

He tipped slowly back in his chair, and stretched out his legs, his feet finding their habitual home on the edge of his desk. 'What would get me motivated to start my job search in earnest?' he wondered. 'And what type of job would I be most excited to move into?' He closed his eyes for a moment, and his mind drifted, as he tried to visualise a happy outcome . . .

Unexpectedly yet tentatively, the door opened, and his old school-friend Joe appeared. He looked happy, fit and well-dressed. Father of three, husband of one, and owner of several companies, he had done well for himself. After a short conversation, Joe glanced at his watch and had to leave – an important meeting to attend.

'Good old Joe,' muttered Alex, 'he always was cut out for success.' Jealousy surged within him.

He reached over to the phone to ask his secretary why she had not let him know that Joe would be coming in. But it rang before he could pick it up.

'Just checking your reservation for this evening, sir.' Alex liked that word "sir". Especially when it came from the most up-market and difficult-to-book restaurant in town. Alex confirmed the reservation, and on a whim, perhaps inspired by his recent jealousy, asked for the best table in the house. As a regular, he was obliged. Alex liked Power.

'Julia: no more unexpected calls, please,' he called over his shoulder to his secretary in the adjoining office.

He saw that in the office car park, top salesman Dave was climbing into his Ferrari, off for lunch with the extremely attractive woman whose long legs were unlikely to fit into the car. Alex decided that he shouldn't think about sex while in the office. It was incompatible with the company's statement of mission and values – and Alex had helped to draft them. His sense of Duty overcame his sense of Lust.

He started to think again about his job search. His first employer sprang to mind – the manager of the Greasy Spoon café where Alex had spent several summer vacation breaks from school. 'You're really well suited to waiting tables,' the manager had said. 'In fact I can't see you ever doing much else, you just don't seem smart enough.' All those years ago, Alex had resolved to show him and all the others in his small home town just how successful he could be. Pride could be a good motivator.

His mind drifted off to the castle he had just bought. It had thirty-five rooms, a moat and a draw-bridge. He entered the castle and paced the grounds. He climbed to the highest turret, went outside to the battlements and surveyed his lands. 'I like having money,' he thought.

Just at that moment, he heard a noise of stone moving against stone. He felt his feet giving way. He saw small cracks appearing in the part of the battlements on which he was standing. Suddenly he was falling, accelerating towards the moat. His life flashed before him. He cursed the money which had bought him the castle. He was about to hit the ground . . .

*   *   *

. . . Alex awoke as his feet slipped off the desk and hit the floor with a heel-numbing and knee-straightening thud.

This time, the telephone really did ring. It was Julia. 'Sorry to disturb you, but I have your wife on the line . . . and don't forget the meeting with the project team in half an hour.'

'Hi, Sarah. Is everything OK?'

'Yes, Alex. I just rang to say that I . . . I . . . I lo . . .'

'What? What?' asked a tantalised Alex, to whom Sarah, for some time, had not declared her love.

Sarah sneezed, then continued, 'I . . . I lost the address for the restaurant where we're meeting tonight. The others want to meet us there. Where is it again?'

Alex, crestfallen, supplied the relevant details.

'Oh yes,' said Sarah, 'one more thing: I think I love you.'

They both laughed, and Alex was surprised to find that he was happy for the rest of the day. He thought about the images and urges which had visited him during his dream, and some of them retained their attraction.

But he realised that what really got his motivation going again was the Love he shared with his wife, and the prospect of Respect with which he hoped his team would come to regard him.

In addition, he resolved to identify what factors generated a similar impetus in each of his team members.

21

Impetus

A compelling vision is all very well. But what if we're *not really motivated to become motivated!?* Or what if someone else, whom we want to help, has this condition?

Firstly, you will need to reach deeper inside yourself – to find some motivating factor which is even more inspiring than a vision of successfully completing the task at hand. You will need to find the basis for an internal selling job, to convince yourself to act – to create impetus and to overcome inertia and procrastination.

Perhaps for you – or for the person you want to motivate – 'money makes the world go round'. But this is unlikely to be the full story.

The facing page sets out some potential motivators. Some might appear more 'healthy' than others; but each can be used in either 'good' or 'bad' ways. Just remember that you tend to reap what you sow! See also the 'hierarchy of needs' (Chapter 10).

Secondly, you might kick-start your VICTORY loop with a simple one-page plan – just a list of a few steps to get you going. You don't need the full plot – you'll add to your plan later, but at least you've 'started the engine'.

* * *

Successful motivators know how to create impetus.

Source of Impetus

MONEY: *'If I do this, I'll make a lot of money and everything will be OK.'*
. . . but for most people, money is merely a 'hygiene' factor: if they feel 'rewarded fairly', and reasonably secure, then prospects of modest additional financial rewards do not motivate strongly.
For others, money is the ultimate measure of success.

POWER: *'Achieving this will allow me to control others, or my environment.'*
Most people want some power over their lives. For some people, 'enough power' is 'a modest degree of influence'.
Others want more and stop only when they fully control their relationships, teams, countries or worlds. Such people often believe that only they can keep things well organised: 'Chaos will reign if I relinquish power.' Or they may just see power as a way of 'keeping score'.

SEX: *'Accomplishing this will make me more sexually attractive.'*
. . . but we need to guard against misjudging what will turn our mate on.

ENVY: *'I want what he's got.'*
. . . more constructively: 'If he can do it, I can do it better.'

PRIDE: *'They said I could never do it – I'll show them!'*
. . . and then you do!

DUTY: *'I have to do this, because I'm a good husband, wife, son, daughter, worker, boss, friend . . .'*
. . . duty is 'good', but can be a defence mechanism (see chapter 10).

GROWTH, SUCCESS: *'I made it! (And now I'm ready for my next challenge.)'*
. . . In the land of motivation, nothing succeeds like success.

HOPE: *Without hope, there is no motivation.*

OTHER MOTIVATORS: *respect, sibling rivalry, altruism, patriotism, creed, etc.*

23

With a well-turned phrase, Bob ruins Zadok's day.

**Many things affect confidence
– even a few simple words**

5. Confidence

In which Alex helps Rob to build faith in his abilities and in himself

As Project Excalibur started in earnest, the team urgently needed an initial, 'quick and dirty' version of the customer complaints data. It was Rob's role to produce this, structured into whatever groupings were most readily available from the information already in the computer.

Although the other team members could make a start on their own parts of the project, ultimately everyone was relying on that initial cut of the data to make their efforts more focused.

Kate, for example, was going to interview some of the major corporate buyers of the company's products. While she could set up the interviews, she couldn't prepare the detailed interview questions without having a structured list of the complaints. Bill and Emma needed similar guidance to follow up some of the more frequent complaints with the relevant departments within the company. And Jerry needed the information to assess the financial implications for the company of the apparent product and service problems. The team therefore needed Rob's work urgently, but Rob's progress in the last week appeared slow.

Alex thought it time to investigate. He looked up Rob's previous personnel records and talked to the person who had managed Rob before his move to Special Projects. It appeared that Rob had performed well during his first project with the company, several years earlier. Then his performance had – slowly but surely – declined.

Alex was unsure whether to tackle Rob's current lack of progress in 'working hours', or in a less formal setting. He chose a middle path, deciding to take Rob out for a quick lunch, during which Rob might be more open about himself.

'So, Rob, how's the progress on that initial cut of the data?'

'Nearly finished – a few more days and it should be ready,' came Rob's familiar reply.

'That's what you said a few days ago, Rob. We've arrived at a stage where the rest of the team needs the information, otherwise they'll just be spinning their wheels.'

Alex suspected that Rob lacked confidence, despite his cheery exterior. He recalled the recent advice that Michael, his mentor, had given when they had met during the previous week:

> *Even with a strong vision of success, a person whose confidence is low will probably neither set, nor 'go for', stretching challenges. And then he or she will not reap the energising rewards of receiving praise for strong performance. The VICTORY loop will be broken – permanently.*
>
> *If you're building someone's confidence, you first need to establish the right context: try to build their trust and show that the person's confidence and success is something about which you* care. *Then cultivate this confidence as you would cultivate a garden: seed the confidence with vision and your strongly stated belief that the person will be successful in their venture; feed the confidence with praise for those parts of the job which have been well done, and encourage the person to acknowledge their own efforts and to praise themselves; then help the person to* weed *out negative 'self-talk' which they themselves – or others – generate. You can apply these principles to building your own confidence, as well as to building the confidence of others.*

Alex asked Rob which parts of his work in the last week had gone well and in which parts he was experiencing problems with which Alex or others could help him. Having started to build Rob's trust, Alex broadened the discussion to ask Rob frankly about his previous two years with the company. Why had his performance apparently declined rather than improved?

It turned out that Rob did lack confidence – in many areas of his life. When he had been moved to Special Projects, his confidence had taken a further knock.

'Rob, I want you to be able to look back on this project as the best piece of work you've ever done. I'll help you, and I know you can do it – that's why I really liked that vision of you as Merlin the Magician. You know you can be a wizard with the numbers. Now, let's get practical: tell me what you think has gone well over the past few weeks and in what areas you could do with my help.'

Rob couldn't think of many things which he had done well so far, so Alex had to help him recall a few examples, both from his current – and from his previous – work.

'I suppose I did do a reasonable job in those areas,' admitted Rob grudgingly.

'As you were able to accomplish all those other tasks, Rob, I'm sure you can sort out the current problem with the data on Project Excalibur. In fact, I know you can do it and *you* know you can do it. I want you to get that data to the team by the end of tomorrow. And when you've done it, I want you to add that success to your stockpile of confidence-building memories!'

Rob thought this was a somewhat strange conversation to be having with his 'boss', but he did start to feel more confident.

* * *

In his interactions with Rob over the next few weeks, Alex continued to focus on building Rob's confidence. He also suggested that Rob log for himself, every few days, the tasks which he had completed particularly well. Alex reviewed this list with Rob from time to time and re-inforced – where appropriate – the positive messages.

* * *

It didn't happen overnight, but Rob's confidence did grow – and with it the level of initiative which he took.

It had required Alex to make some investment during the early stages of Project Excalibur, but it paid off in many ways. Alex found that Rob required much less of his time later in the project, so that Alex could focus more on his own job search; Alex had reminded himself of the major lessons regarding the building of confidence and applied them to *himself* occasionally; and somehow the team members ended up supporting each other and mutually building their confidence, in ways which Alex had never envisioned.

Building Confidence

'Con-fidence' comes from the Latin meaning 'with faith'. How do we build our faith in ourselves – faith that we can accomplish a specific result, faith that we can become a particular type of person? How do we build other people's confidence in themselves?

Confidence is a garden which needs seeding, feeding, and weeding:

- **Seeding.** This is where the Vision plays a vital role. By merely daring to germinate the seeds of a vision of success, we have taken the first step towards building confidence. By daring ourselves or others to be *great* the journey has started. Create and revisit your vision to build and sustain confidence.

  Even your act of turning up as a gardener (and thus demonstrating that you care about the person's confidence) will do much to help build it.

- **Feeding.** No garden can grow in a vacuum. Each garden needs the right type of fertiliser, enough sun, sufficient water. Not surprisingly, the most frequent source of nourishment for our confidence is potentially the **positive feedback** received (from one's self or from others) as a result of our efforts (see Chapter 8). Make sure you get (and give) enough of it! Find ways to acknowledge your own successes.

  Remember to engage your body and spirit, as well as your mind. Keep physically fit; listen to enlivening music; successfully indulge in your favourite pastimes.

- **Weeding.** All too easily, the gardens of our confidence can become overrun by weeds which entangle and by pests which consume. These confidence-busters take various forms, as we'll explore later in this book (e.g. Chapter 10 on psychology and defence mechanisms; Chapter 12 on fear of success). Know your vermin and banish them.

Confidence

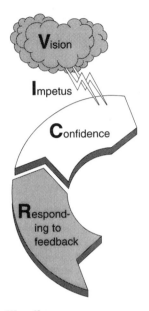

Tend confidence, as a garden

1. Seeding
- Revisit your vision periodically.
- Embellish it when needed, to make it more powerful.
- Recall your previous successes.

2. Feeding
- Talk with people who will praise you for things done well.
- Take time to acknowledge your own successes.
- Cross-pollinate confidence in your mission by reflecting on successes in other areas of your life.
- Use physical exercise, music or other fertilisers to help you feel good about yourself.

3. Weeding
- Catalogue the weeds and vermin which you know can undermine your confidence; eradicate these pests and impostors (e.g. spending time with people who put you or others down; self-deprecation; being so busy that you do not take time out for yourself – and therefore feeling that you are someone's puppet).

Note: when providing encouraging praise to other people, address the points made in Chapter 17.

Exercise

Become a gardener:

- Identify your (or others') habits of seeding, feeding and weeding confidence.

- Play with this metaphor for yourself; what gardening tools do you – or could you – use? Do you take time to smell the roses?

As Ned Belsky hesitates, Neil Armstrong
becomes the *first* man on the moon.

**Seize the moment, not the
uncertainty**

6. Taking the Plunge

In which Alex helps someone to 'go for it'

'Uncle Alex, look at *me*!' Alex's six-year old nephew, Jack, was perching precariously on the edge of the pool. His arms windmilled wildly, but he had no intention *whatsoever* of overbalancing and falling in from the pool side's dizzy height of six inches above the water.

'Very clever,' acknowledged Alex sarcastically, 'but isn't it about time that you learned to *dive* in?'

'I can so dive in,' was Jack's immediate response.

'Go on then, show me.'

'You've got to be with a teacher if you want to dive in. They said so at school.'

Alex had met Jack's headmistress only once, when standing in for Jack's parents at a parent-teacher evening. Having taken an instant dislike to her, he now resolved to conspire with Jack in flouting this ill-founded rule. *He*'d show Jack how to dive, in full public view.

Recognising Jack's previous claim of diving skill for the bluff that it was, Alex launched straight into the lesson. He adopted the semi-crouched position – with arms extended forwards – which uncles are genetically primed to assume on such occasions. A few minutes later, with Jack determinedly interested in something at the other end of the pool, Alex's legs started to tire and he decided on a different approach.

For some reason, that simplistic VICTORY model popped up in his mind. 'I wonder if it would work in a swimming pool? Vision, confidence, taking the plunge . . . Let's start with some vision and some confidence and repeat them a few times,' he thought.

Alex knew that Jack shared the family trait of enjoying the act of breaking rules – at least minor ones. 'Let's do something that the teacher says we're not allowed to do,' he ventured. Hardly a compelling vision (perhaps just as well), but it did secure Jack's attention.

Alex coaxed Jack through some preparations. 'Let's see how big a splash you can make just jumping in . . . WOW . . . those kids are making *big* splashes, I bet you can't make an *even* bigger one . . .' Jack's confidence seemed to be growing, though he wasn't really building his skills at diving.

'OK, Jack, now let's *dive* in.' This transition to the main objective was not as deft as Alex had thought it was and Jack ran to grab his fluorescent green-and-pink-super-turbo-Exocet-water-blaster-gun instead.

It occurred to Alex that he might have uncovered an additional and potentially show-stopping obstacle – Jack did not like getting his head wet. Somehow, Alex managed to help Jack over this particular phobia. Now was the time to really go for it.

'Jack, what's your favourite animal?'

'Simba the lion, from *Lion King* – what's yours?'

'Superman,' replied Alex.

'That's not an animal, that's a man. I like Simba because he can roar and jump off high cliffs.'

Jack's response gave Alex cause for hope. They got down on all fours and became lions, with louder and louder roars and wilder and wilder swipes at each other. All of a sudden, Alex roared and dived headlong into the pool.

Equally suddenly, Jack didn't like this game any more. With childish insight, he decided that there was something fishy going on.

It took a further fifteen minutes, but eventually Alex convinced Jack that Jack *was* Simba. He could roar, he could leap, and he could . . . dive. And it worked. He dived in. Then, with a nonchalance found only in infants, Jack spent the next five minutes trading on this just-discovered skill as if he had always possessed it. Whenever he wanted to dive in, he just became Simba and roared. He had a vision, he had confidence and he had a trigger for action – the roar.

But trouble was in store. 'Uncle Alex, have you ever dived in off that big high place?'

Alex glanced nervously over his shoulder at the thirty-metre-high springboard. 'Lots of times,' he lied.

'Go on then, show me.'

'Not now, it's time to leave.'

'Just *once*?' pleaded Jack.

'Go on, just once,' came a mischievous voice from a few yards away. Alex turned to see Mark, competitive swimmer and Alex's brother-in-law.

'Yes, Uncle Alex, just be Superman, like you said – just shout "kryptonite" and everything will be OK.' Their surprise visitor arched an eyebrow.

Confident of gait but not of gut, Alex strode to the ladder which led to the diving board, furtively checked that it was properly attached to the concrete structure, and ascended. Then he found himself on the edge. There were only two things which could now save him from a literal and embarrassingly visible climbdown. One was the vision of a caped yet non-existent film character. The other was that line he had programmed to appear when faced with risk: 'Just be *at least* a little bit adventurous'.

During his thirty-metre fall, he thanked God for a life well lived and cursed the speed at which children learn.

* * *

Drying himself in the changing room afterwards, Alex reflected that even adults regress – at least partly – to a childlike state when faced with sufficiently daunting challenges. In these situations, he mused, the triggers for decisive action can appear from most unlikely sources – from visionary pictures of oneself, from pre-programmed phrases, or even from unexpected visitors.

Taking the Plunge

'The moment comes. We grasp the opportunity. We commit to action with vim and vigour. Our determination brooks no quarter. We dismiss nay-sayers. Surmount unscalable obstacles. Throw irresistible forces into reverse. Succeed. Reward our selves.'

Or: *'We dither. Fiddle. Sort of try. With half or three-quarters of our heart, we have a go.'*

Why do we end up on one of these courses and not on the other? Why do our twilight thoughts conjure up the former image of success, while the morning reduces us to sober hesitancy (or vice versa)? Why do we brake ourselves at that last moment?

This entire book helps you to examine and resolve these issues from a number of angles.* At this point, however, there are three points to keep in mind:

- **Preparation for the plunge.** Whatever the plunge which you secretly want to take, your chances of success increase astronomically if you have a) developed a compelling vision for yourself, b) mustered the relevant support from others, and c) chosen your timing for action wisely.

- **Plunging.** At the point of no return, a voice must speak to you – literally. The facing page offers statements, one or more of which you may choose to programme for automatic emergence in times of need.

- **Post-plunge.** Reflect on whether the plunge was really as frightening as you had expected. Perhaps you can grow to enjoy the adrenalin which accompanies initiative.

* * *

Hesitancy can break the VICTORY cycle. Avoid it at all costs.

---

*Especially Chapters 3 (Vision), 5 (Confidence), 8 (Responding to Feedback), 12 (Fear of Success), 16 (NLP), 20 (Mastery of Motivation).

Overcoming Hesitation

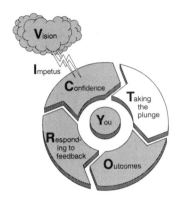

Be, at least, just a bit adventurous.
Alex

The more I fail, the luckier I am!
Anonymous

Learn to fail better.
Samuel Beckett

*Good judgement is the result
of experience. And experience
is the result of bad judgement.*
Walter Wriston, Chairman of Citicorp

*The mind is its own place, and in itself
Can make a heav'n of hell, a hell of heav'n.*
Milton

*The speeding arrow, the passing second, and the missed opportunity –
the things which can never be brought back.*
Anonymous

*Come fill the Cup, and in the Fire of Spring
The Winter Garment of Repentance fling:
For The Bird of Time has but a little way
To fly – and Lo! the Bird is on the Wing.*
Omar Khayyam

Macbeth: If we should fail?
Lady Macbeth: We, fail! But screw your courage to the sticking-place, and
we'll not fail.
Shakespeare

Exercise

Find your personal anecdotal antidote to hesitancy:

- **Programme an image or saying to pop up automatically at the moments of truth.**

Professor Grimes had invented the perfect stumbling block, but now found himself helpless in its cruel grasp . . .

Acknowledge your successes
and mine confidence from
them; see setbacks as
blessings to be unmasked

7. Observing Outcomes and Seeing Obstacles as Opportunities

In which Alex tries to keep things in perspective

Alex forgot all about his successful adventures in the swimming pool as he arrived at work the next day. Lightning had struck during the night and the resulting power surge had scrambled the data stored on the team's hard disc. All the information on the thousands of customer complaints had been wiped out.

The team was worried and so was Alex. In reality, their worry was caused more by their uncertainty about the implications than by any certain knowledge that the project would fail utterly. But the worry was real.

Alex felt in need of some counsel and managed to track down Michael by phone, '. . . so how on earth do you keep people motivated in the face of disaster?' he asked.

'Napoleon made an entire career of using disasters to motivate people,' joked Michael, with annoying breeziness. But he continued more helpfully, 'OK, Alex, here are some thoughts on obstacles – and on "outcomes" more generally, as they relate to the role of the leader and motivator.

'First, you really do need to adopt the mindset that *any* obstacle can be overcome. But *in addition* you need to believe – because it is always true – that the creativity which you apply in working around the obstacle will generate ideas that will actually allow the project to proceed *even better* than if you hadn't encountered the obstacle!

'You'll be forced to examine options *which you could have thought of in the first place*, but which – for some reason – you didn't think of. In that sense, apparent obstacles are a blessing in disguise – provided that you can unmask that disguise. For example, as you tackle the problem of the data which has been lost from the computer, you should aim to find initiatives that will allow you and the team to reach a better outcome for the project *overall*. The more that you genuinely believe this, the better the initiatives that will emerge. Envision any obstacle as a divine messenger. You can choose to shoot the messenger, or to extract the secret meaning which she bears.

'This mindset of "earned serendipity" is important for the leader's own motivation, and for the team's resulting confidence and motivation, too.

'Second, make sure that you are seeing the apparent obstacle from an advantageous viewpoint. Link back to the overall visions which you developed for the project, for the mission and for the team members (including yourself). Is it really a mountain which confronts you or a molehill? Perhaps it's a foothill? Using the correct perspective will help you to stay balanced and therefore more able to generate creative solutions.

'Third, recognise that the best plans are malleable plans. Don't chastise yourself for devising a plan which lacked perfect foresight. Rather, congratulate yourself on reworking that plan to take advantage of serendipity.

'By the way, Alex, there's a point which I should have mentioned last month when we were discussing visions and plans. I've noticed that some people develop plans which are structured in a way which makes them very difficult ever to change. Other people develop plans which are intrinsically more malleable. You might take this opportunity to check on your plan for the overall project – is the plan simultaneously definite yet malleable?

'And one final point . . . I've talked about outcomes which are *obstacles*. Unfortunately, we usually pay more attention to them than we do to *successes*. It may not be relevant for you at the moment, but do look out for positive things which you, or the team, are achieving as the project progresses. And then deliver some congratulations! Success breeds success. True leaders are excellent breeders!'

Alex finished jotting down Michael's points of advice, thanked him and then started chewing the end of his pencil. What would be his next step?

*　*　*

To cut a long story short, Alex worked with the team – and particularly with Rob (who had been in charge of the now non-existent data), using Michael's suggestions.

Things were indeed as bad as they had at first seemed – the bits of data had been transformed into random strings of ones and zeros. However, with a little creativity they found a way around the problem. Since Rob had printed out the data at various stages during the past week, the data *did* still exist – but only on paper. In his guise as Merlin the Magician, Rob conjured up the data files, recreating them from the pages which he fed through an optical scanner. It took some effort to harness the power of the scanning program, but it paid off. The team had its data back.

Alex set the team another challenge, so that it would forever remember that: of obstacles are indeed born opportunities. How could they use this experience *to improve the overall results* of the project?

Eventually they hit on a few ideas. They wanted to ensure that future customer comments could be easily captured and logged.

Why not use the scanning idea to get the data directly into the computer? But while scanners could read typefaces, most would still be incapable of reading customers' handwriting. Why not extend the scanning idea – set up a website on the Internet on which customers could log their comments directly? They came up with a few more ideas, recording them for future reference.

They also revisited the overall project plan, and resequenced it to minimise the knock-on impact that possible future 'disasters' in one area might have on other areas.

Outcomes and Obstacles

The fourth step of the VICTORY cycle is about observing Outcomes which result from our initiatives or from our 'taking the plunge', and overcoming Obstacles. Let's focus on the *outcomes and obstacles themselves* rather than the *ways in which we interpret feedback about them* (covered in Chapter 7).

What are the important points about Outcomes and Obstacles as they relate to motivation?

- **Link back to your Vision.** As for all the steps in the VICTORY cycle, keep asking, 'How does this outcome or event relate to the longer-term vision?'

- **Have a plan and a fall-back plan.** In fleshing out the vision of *what* was to be achieved, you developed images of *how* to make progress: the path to success. You should already have translated your image of this path to success into a plan of action. To derive maximum motivational value from your outcomes (however successful they are), make sure you know where they fit into your overall plan.

- **Revise plans into simple jigsaw puzzles, not complex Rubik's cubes.** If your plans are very sequential ('Do A before B, and B before C', like solving a Rubik's cube), then you do not allow yourself much flexibility. But if your plans are more like a jigsaw puzzle, you can make swifter progress. You have greater flexibility: you can work on whichever part makes most sense at the time.

- **Develop serendipity.** Serendipity is the art of turning chance happenings to advantage. By definition, chance happenings are not on anyone's plan. But you can plan to have a bed prepared for the surprise arrival of the guest, Luck.

- **Think small, not just big.** Every culture and every age has many versions of the saying, 'Every journey starts with a step.'

* * *

Learn to see positive outcomes as steps towards your goal. One of the greatest motivators is progress itself. And view every setback as an opportunity to generate a better outcome for the broader mission.

Outcomes, Obstacles and Luck

A Sufi dervish who had travelled the desert for many years finally came upon an oasis of civilisation – a village called Sandy Hills.

In search of lodging, he was directed to the ranch of the wealthy Shakir, whose name means 'one who thanks the Lord constantly'. Shakir's riches exceeded even those of his neighbour Haddad.

After spending several days as Shakir's guest, the dervish departed and thanked his host, adding, 'Thank God that you are well off.'

'But, dervish,' replied Shakir, 'don't be fooled by appearances, for this too shall pass.'

As he journeyed far and wide, the dervish puzzled over the meaning of this phrase. Five years later he found himself back in Sandy Hills, but Shakir's house and ranch had disappeared. The locals directed the dervish to the house of Haddad, the neighbour. 'What happened?' asked the dervish, as Shakir emerged in rags.

'My ranch was destroyed by flood, though Haddad's was not. Haddad took pity on me and I am now his servant, but this too shall pass . . .'

Many miles and several years later, the dervish returned to find Shakir, finely dressed, welcoming him at the entrance to Haddad's ranch. 'Haddad died several years ago and, having no heir, left his estate to me. But this too shall pass . . .'

One day, the dervish had news that Shakir had passed away. Returning to Sandy Hills to visit Shakir's grave, the dervish found his tombstone inscribed with the words, 'This too shall pass.'

And so it was, some time later, that the dervish was to win the competition which the king had mounted. The king wanted something which would make him sad if he was too happy and happy if he became sad.

The dervish presented the king with a ring, on the inside of which were inscribed the words, 'This too shall pass.'

Fariduddin Attar (1136–1230)

Bob began to wonder if his '*Pants protect you from feedback*' strategy was sustainable.

Wake up! Look, listen, learn, interpret. Cancel negative self-talk

8. Responding to Feedback

In which Alex helps to prevent Kate from undermining herself

Now starting its second month, Project Excalibur was well under way. The team had identified the main types of problem about which customers were complaining. Kate had embarked on her round of interviews with the more important customers, to see how those problems could be resolved.

Kate had seemed the ideal team member for this role. She was outgoing and up-beat, with a natural enthusiasm for fixing things.

A week into the interviews, however, she came to see Alex. 'I don't think I can take any more of this,' she started. 'These interviews are very stressful and I think I'm causing more problems than I'm solving.' Alex was surprised and asked Kate to tell him a bit more about the interviews.

'I always leave the interviews feeling really depressed. I know I ought to be using those discussions to solve the customer's problems. Instead, I end up just sitting there while the customer moans on and on. They ought to treat me with more respect, but eventually they just say that they've got to leave and the meeting ends. And during the interviews I always forget to ask the right questions, even though I've written them down in advance . . .'

Alex thought he knew what was happening here, but he let Kate continue, noting a few points as she spoke. He knew that she was actually doing an excellent job on the interviews. He'd seen the notes which she had written up after the meetings. He'd even had a call from one of the customers to thank the company for making the effort of arranging a personal visit (although he'd forgotten to mention the call to Kate and kicked himself for that).

Kate remained in full flow for another five minutes, so Alex eventually interrupted. 'Kate. First, I want you to know that you're doing an excellent job on the interviews.' He explained that the meeting notes were very helpful and he mentioned the telephone call which he'd received from the customer. He knew that Kate would probably just think he was trying to calm her down. So he demonstrated in a tangible way the positive nature of his feedback, by explaining that he definitely wanted her to continue with the interviews – she was conducting them so well.

Then Alex looked down at the scrap of paper on which he had been jotting a few points.

'There is only one problem with the interviewing, Kate. It's *not a problem of the interviews themselves*. It's *a problem with the way that you are viewing your ability to conduct them*. You are choosing to hear and view the feedback from yourself and from others in a way which *undermines* your confidence, rather than *builds it*.

'It's the ultimate irony: you do a great job, but you convince yourself that you're doing a lousy job. The problem is that this irony will lead to tragedy if you don't fix it.'

He explained by sketching out the VICTORY cycle: our confidence (and from there our likelihood of taking further constructive action) depends more on the way in which we *interpret* the feedback from the results of our efforts than on the *results* themselves, or even than the *feedback* itself!

'But how do you change the way you interpret feedback?' asked Kate.

'Well, in the first place you need to ensure that you are actually receiving enough feedback – or information – from the "environment". It sounds obvious, but it's amazing how often we don't do this. Take the example of your customer interviews: the only thing to which you were responding was your "self-talk" – things you were telling yourself. If you were worried, you could have asked me how well I thought the interviews were proceeding. That might have reminded me to mention the grateful call from the customer, too.'

'OK, Alex, but suppose I'm receiving the feedback – how do I then change the way I respond to it? I think that was your main point.'

Alex continued, 'You have to monitor your self-talk (if necessary, rewriting the scripts which you continually use on yourself), and you need to examine your beliefs – your models of how you think the world is, or should be.

'Let me give you some examples. When you started to explain the problems you were having, you used the word "ought" twelve times, "must" six times and "always" four times.

'When you said, "I *always* forget to ask the right questions", you were probably being inaccurate. I'm sure you asked the right questions much of the time. Telling yourself that you always do something poorly is a generalisation which will ultimately destroy your confidence. Try, therefore, to script yourself with more positive (and probably more accurate) self-dialogue.'

Alex then went on to show Kate that we all hold implicit beliefs about how the world works. Beliefs can be rational and lead to 'healthy' emotions and constructive actions. But beliefs can also be irrational (usually based on a plethora of 'shoulds', 'oughts', 'musts' and 'alwayses'). Irrational beliefs tend to produce unhealthy emotions such as anxiety and depression, which in turn lead to ineffective or destructive actions such as abuse of others, self-abuse and procrastination. Alex tried to make the point more clearly by sketching out a diagram.*

'Kate, from what I've seen, I think you're a bit of a perfectionist. Obviously, we want you to do as good a job as possible. But if you believe that every single interview has to be absolutely perfect, then I'm concerned that you'll become so disappointed with yourself that you'll lose your confidence and concentration and then start to screw up.

'Anyway, give it some thought, and let me know if you'd like me to go with you to the next interview.'

Kate realised that she could not hope actually to *solve* many of the customers' problems during the interviews and set herself the more achievable goal of *understanding* the customers' complaints as fully as possible. The next interview went well and she didn't need to take up Alex's offer to accompany her. She forgot to congratulate herself (but she remembered to do so on the subsequent occasion).

---

*This diagram is reproduced on page 47.

Responding to Feedback

Responding to feedback is how we close the VICTORY loop of motivation and refuel our supplies of confidence.

Feedback is the prime source of our learning, development and motivation. It lets us stay on course as we captain the ship of ourselves. Amazingly, many people discourage, avoid, misinterpret and ignore it – either consciously or by using more subtle ploys. However, let's assume that we, others, or the environment are providing us with information (feedback) about something we are doing or have completed;* let's focus on interpreting and responding to that feedback.

- **Develop your appetite for bitter-sweetness.** Successful people use the sweetness of positive feedback to build directly their confidence and motivation. But they have also learned to enjoy the more bitter fruits of feedback from their *less successful* labours to enhance their skills.

- **Re-script your self-talk.** 'Why am I so stupid?' is not something which successful people say to themselves. 'What were the factors which led me to that decision? How might I do things differently next week?' might be. This is a large and subtle topic, the key points of which are summarised on the opposite page.

- **Refocus your beliefs.** Our beliefs are the lenses through which we see the world. Check that they do not distort (see opposite).

- **Praise yourself.** When is the last time that you rewarded (or even acknowledged [or even noticed explicitly]) some success which you achieved?

---

*For help on soliciting and giving feedback, see Landsberg, *The Tao of Coaching*, pages 10–15 and 20–5.

Self-Talk and Beliefs

Self-talk – we need to avoid three traps as we try to groove healthier dialogues with ourselves:

Trap	Description	Example
Generalise	Subtly telling yourself that you have an intrinsic negative trait	'I'm always forgetting everything.'
Irrationalise	Drawing conclusions which the facts do not necessarily support	'My boss didn't congratulate me on my paper, so I must have omitted something.'
Transpose	Using negative feelings about one area of your life, to infect other areas	'I can't write well, so I won't be a good public speaker.'

Beliefs: These are the lenses through which we see the world. 'Rational' beliefs trigger healthy emotions and constructive action. 'Irrational' beliefs lead to destructive action. The ideas are drawn from Ellis's Rational Emotive Behaviour Therapy.

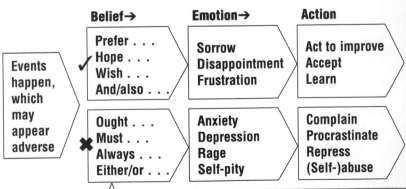

E.g. 'I *must always* be respected; if someone puts me down then it's *terrible* and *awful*: I'll have to hide (or beat them up).'

Exercise

• Use Appendix D to examine your self-talk and your beliefs.

47

Colin hesitated, overcome by an intensely felt need to contemplate the meaning of life and the nature of self.

Harness visceral urges to transform yourself positively

9. You

As he drove to work the next morning, Alex felt that he was now propelling Project Excalibur with sufficient momentum. Kate was making better progress with the customer interviews; Rob was starting to analyse the data, and the other team members were in active discussion with the divisions which handled production and product development.

Alex arrived at his desk. As he flipped open his briefcase, two beer mats popped out. They bore the pearls of wisdom which Michael had penned several months ago. Alex glanced at Michael's picture of the VICTORY model, and was somehow surprised that he seemed to have adopted that way of thinking about motivation, almost as second nature.

Only one thing bothered him – he could not remember Michael having said much about the final 'Y' in the picture. He recalled that the 'Y' stood for 'You', but that was all Michael had said.

Perhaps that was appropriate, thought Alex. After all, it is up to each of us to define what we want to be. And much of what we are is determined by the degree to which – and direction *in* which – we are motivated by ourselves and by others.

Alex's schedule for the day was too busy to allow him to philosophise. But a line from Nietzsche sprang unbidden from his memory: '*We are as happy as we decide to be.*' Alex wondered if that was because we are as *motivated* as we decide to be.

Alex checked his diary and decided to postpone further thoughts on this until after the evening lecture on psychology for which he had reluctantly signed up. His reluctance was due to his uncertainty – shared by many of his managerial colleagues – about whether psychology was of any relevance to the business world. He hoped that a 'Rough Guide' to the subject would prove his cynicism ill-founded.

You

At the heart of the VICTORY cycle lies a 'You'. This is the person whom you are motivating – yourself, a friend or a colleague.

Obviously, this 'You' is defined, characterised and created by many things. But the elements of the VICTORY cycle referred to in previous chapters play a particularly critical role. Our visions for ourselves, our levels of confidence, etc., in some senses define who and what we are.

Perhaps more important than the simple sum of these elements is the power of the connections between them: many are the visions which we never get around to realising, often there is an impetus – but it is bottled up, creating anxiety.

As a result, the skill of motivation involves helping someone to *see, create and strengthen the links between the steps*. Helping someone to create a vision of their future success is good; but encouraging them to relate this vision to some deeper impetus has a better chance of producing action. Helping someone to feel more confident is good; but supporting – or pushing – them to actually take the plunge is better still.

* * *

The great artist does not just paint with virtuosity individual trees, rivers and people. He also has a way of linking these elements in a way which is called his *style*.

In the same way, the great motivator does not just address topics such as vision and confidence in a standalone manner. He also helps the person he is motivating to develop or enhance their own individual style, by helping him to integrate these elements in a coherent way.

The Heart of the VICTORY cycle

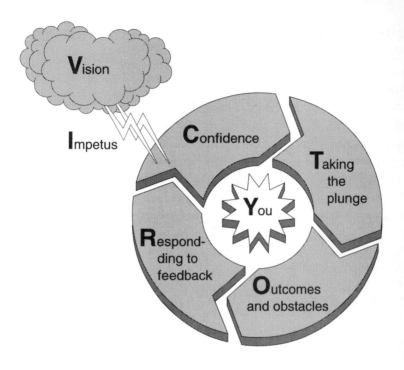

Fang's ambition to become Sheepdog Champion of the World was frustrated by his deep misunderstanding of sheep psychology.

Know yourself – and others, too

10. Essential Psychology

A distillation of a hundred years' thinking on what makes people tick

Alex shuffled into the lecture room. He timed his entrance late enough to allow him to hide among his colleagues at the back of the room, but not so late that he'd be forced to sit at the front.

He'd been intrigued to hear of this presentation on the essentials of psychology and thought it would tie in with his new interest in motivation.

He had 'signed up' via the Human Resources department and now waited to hear what Dr Bea Kaplan – eminent psychologist and counsellor to the company – had to offer.

* * *

Later, when she had finished, he had found her words so interesting that he took away with him a copy of the ten-page outline of her talk:

Essential Psychology for the Layman

Dr Bea Kaplan, MA, MD

Psychology is the study of what makes people tick. Of all careers, that of manager or leader requires the greatest understanding of this topic.

Managers are permanently surrounded by many people of widely differing personalities and with whom they often have not necessarily chosen to spend time. And with these people the manager must interact in an exceptionally wide variety of ways: directing, advising, asking, telling, coaching, socialising, training, congratulating, motivating.

This article therefore aims to help you understand the essentials of psychology as currently understood, so that you can motivate and interact more effectively with others. It sets out: first, the body of beliefs which is common to most schools of psychology; second, the differing emphases placed by certain schools (such as those of Freud and Jung) in contributing to the development of psychology; and third, the more influential theories of motivation, primarily as they apply in the workplace. The article concludes with a more detailed explanation of two topics: Maslow's hierarchy of needs and defence mechanisms.

What most psychologists agree with

Psychologists of most schools agree on the following five essential principles.

1. **Actions speak louder than words.** Our personalities are characterised and unveiled by the ways in which we respond to specific situations ('stimuli'), or the ways in which we take initiatives when immersed in various environments. Rarely are we so self-aware that we can accurately describe our personality – to ourselves or to others – in words alone.

2. **The pain of trade-offs.** In deciding what actions to take, we make trade-offs. We aim to gratify our urges, yet we avoid making too much trouble for ourselves. More specifically:

   • These *actions* of ours fall into two categories: they are usually either acts of creation or acts of destruction and each type of act can be directed internally (towards ourselves), or externally (towards other people or things). These acts can be either 'active' or 'passive' and often they move us either closer to a person or thing, or away from it – see Exhibit 1.

   • The *urges* which drive these actions spring from our wish to make ourselves or other people more akin to the image we have in mind for us or for them. In most people, these spring from wishes to be

Exhibit 1

TYPES OF ACTION WHICH WE TAKE		

Our actions are creative or destructive, internally or externally directed and active or passive.

	Internally directed	**Externally directed**
Creative	Learning a new skill; self-praise *Accepting others' help*	Helping others; making things *Letting children explore*
Destructive	Self-abuse *Getting out of shape*	Ridiculing others *Letting someone slip up*

Italics = examples of passive acts

Exhibit 2

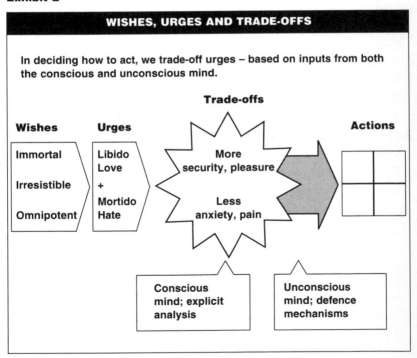

WISHES, URGES AND TRADE-OFFS

In deciding how to act, we trade-off urges – based on inputs from both the conscious and unconscious mind.

Trade-offs

Wishes — Urges — Actions

Immortal / Libido Love / More security, pleasure

Irresistible / + / Less anxiety, pain

Omnipotent / Mortido Hate

Conscious mind; explicit analysis

Unconscious mind; defence mechanisms

a) immortal in being, b) irresistible in charm, and/or c) omnipotent in influence. These wishes are translated into urges and actions by the forces of love (= libido → creation), or hate (= mortido → destruction). See Exhibit 2.

- In *avoiding trouble* for ourselves, we like results which increase security and pleasure and which reduce anxiety and pain. Sometimes we pay attention to these factors in a conscious way. At other times these factors act through our unconscious mind, by way of defence mechanisms such as denial, repression or inappropriate rationalisation (see below).

3. **Regression when stressed.** When confronted with situations that are sufficiently stressful, we tend to fall back (or regress) to behaviours which helped us to cope in the past. At an extreme, we end up acting like children. Different people can withstand differing levels of stress before regressing (by varying amounts).

4. **Growth as grooving *versus* growth as changing.** As we grow – and as we experience new or apparently familiar situations – we recognise patterns, 'grooving' the ways in which we react and make decisions. These 'grooved', automatic, habits save us time and energy. But, ideally, we also keep an open mind so that we can learn new ways to interact with our environments.

5. **The Holi Trinity.** Our minds, bodies and spirits are connected holistically. Psychological (mental) health is intimately connected to physical and spiritual health.

How various schools differ

While most schools of psychology (even those of ancient Greece) would agree with the principles set out above, there are areas in which they differ in emphasis – often radically.

Some schools stress the importance of the conscious mind, while others focus on the unconscious. Some stress the apparently indelible impact of childhood experiences, while others believe our development to be more evenly paced throughout our lives. Perhaps the area of greatest difference is in the method of helping people to change (whether those people are relatively 'normal' or in need of more substantial counselling or treatment). Some schools, such as Freud's, emphasise deep analysis into childhood experiences; others work with the adult 'as he presents himself'.

1. **Sigmund Freud** (1856-1939) was the most formative figure in the last hundred years of psychology. He eventually ascribed particular importance to the *unconscious* mind. In his view, the unconscious mind harbours repressed or forgotten experiences which nevertheless drive many aspects of our behaviour. He attempted to penetrate the unconscious with his technique of *psychoanalysis*, which relied extensively on *free association*. He also emphasised (perhaps over-emphasised) the importance of sexual drive (*libido*).

His model for the structure of the personality has – in various guises – stood the test of time:

- The *Id* represents all instinctive urges. It is primitive, biologically determined, impulsive and operates on the *Pleasure Principle* (obtain pleasure, avoid pain). Unsatisfied urges create tensions and these eventually need to be released via action or fantasy. The *Id* resides in the unconscious part of the mind.

- The *Ego* is seated in the conscious and the unconscious mind. It operates on the *Reality Principle*, recognising the constraints of the outside world and delaying until an appropriate time our urge-gratifying actions. The *Ego* acts as the 'manager' of the self.

- The *Superego* operates partly in the conscious mind, but largely in the unconscious. It represents our model of 'correct' behaviour (the *ego-ideal*), and tries to interrupt our actions that are 'inappropriate' by giving voice to the 'conscience'. When the *Superego* fails in this latter role, we feel *guilt* – people with strong *Superegos* feeling more guilty than others.

Freud believed that these three parts of the personality were largely formed by the age of six (by which time we have moved through Freud's *oral*, *anal* and *phallic* stages). Our job as adults is to recognise our make-up and to cope with it, if necessary by using healthy *defence mechanisms* (see below).

2. **Carl Jung** (1875-1961) eventually broke his association with Freud, feeling that Freud placed too much emphasis on sexual drives and on the role of *repressed* feelings.

Exhibit 3

MAJOR SCHOOLS OF PSYCHOLOGY
(Starting at the roots of the tree)

Humanists. Carl Rogers (1902–87) and others. Empathetic, holistic treatment of person's current problems. Rogers: *Client-Centred Therapy, T-group*
Fritz Pearl: *Gestalt Therapy*
Eric Berne: *Transactional Analysis*

Existentialists. Victor Frankel, R. D. Laing and others. Patients are searching for *meaning* in face of doubts, anxieties and certain death.

Abraham Maslow (1908–70). Man is essentially good. Motivation towards *self-actualisation.*

Erik Erikson (1902–94). *Whole life development* from childhood; specific issues to resolve at each stage.

Anna Freud (1895–1982). *Defence mechanisms*; the individual as autonomous and the ego as strengthenable.

Carl Jung (1875–1961). The *unconscious; archetypes; intro/extroversion*; dreams.

Cognitive therapy (late 1950s). Person as a conscious being, not at the mercy of the unconscious and the world:
Beck's *Cognitive Behaviour Therapy*
Ellis's *Rational Emotive Therapy*
Kelly's *Personal Construct Therapy*

Heinz Kohut. Adult persistence of need to idealise (and be recognised by) parents.

Object Relationists. D. W. Winnicott and others. Focus on the relationship between the person and external *objects* (and people).

Behaviourists. Ivan Pavlov (1849–1936), B. F. Skinner (1904–90). Behaviour – not motivation or unconscious – is key; people are operants which can be *conditioned* and desensitised.

Jean Piaget (1896–1980). Scientific, observational approach to child development.

Alfred Adler (1870–1937). Treating the holistic individual; importance of social and societal interactions; *inferiority complex* enduring from childhood.

Sigmund Freud (1856–1939). Founder of modern psychology – see text for details.

Late 1700s. Growing view that the insane could be cured. Studies in mesmerism, hypnotism, phrenology and brain autopsy.

Ancient Greeks – Hippocrates (mental imbalance caused by physical, not divine influence). **Aristotle** (brain's role in condensing the hot vapours of the heart).

Jung believed that the personality comprised three interacting systems: the *conscious*, the *personal unconscious* and the *collective unconscious*. The conscious mind experiences the world through a mixture of *sensing*, *intuition*, *feeling* and *thinking*. The personal unconscious is similar to Freud's version of the unconscious, though Jung thought it had a more benign influence on us and stressed the role of *dreams* in accessing it. The collective unconscious is the carrier of *archetypes* (such as God, Hero, Fairy Godmother), which influence our thoughts and actions. We all carry a similar gallery of these images, which are somehow embedded psychically in all our minds regardless of our upbringing.

Jung's four aspects of the conscious mind, together with his work on *introversion* and *extroversion* are reflected in many psychological profiling tools in current use – such as the Meyers-Briggs Type Indicator.*

3. **Other Schools.** Freud and Jung had laid the basis for psychology as a science. They had elevated it from the experiments with stage hypnotism of the mid-nineteenth century, and linked it to scientific investigations of the physical brain.

Their contemporaries and immediate followers filled in other corners of the science – Anna Freud refining the theory of defence mechanisms, Jean Piaget focusing on child psychology, etc. (see Exhibit 3).

Subsequent developments in psychology mirrored closely the changes taking place more broadly in the West. As the twentieth century dawned and as the Industrial Revolution flourished, the mind itself came to be regarded increasingly as a machine which could be tuned and conditioned: *Behaviourism* flourished. Partly in reaction to this, the mid-twentieth century brought Carl Rogers and the *Humanistic* school. Their emphasis was on genuine, empathetic understanding of the individual. Subsequent decades have seen a proliferation of schools, which differ primarily in the ways in which they seek to make the individual more 'healthy'.

---

*See pages 69 and 128.

Theories of Motivation

It is in the corporate world that motivation has been most studied, ever since Henry Ford's novel concept of the production line (1896) carried us into the twentieth century. With growing numbers of people working more closely together, in larger groups, on more comparable tasks, the time was ripe for scientific studies of how they could be motivated to achieve corporate goals.

Initially, the **Behaviourists** held sway and the tenets of **Pavlov** and **Skinner** were carried into the workplace. Man moved towards carrots and away from sticks. By paying enough carrots for a particular task, the worker could be motivated to perform better.

Partly in reaction to these overly simple propositions, **Edward Tolman** and other **cognitive** psychologists came to the fore. They believed that we are primarily rational, can choose goals and can consciously modify our behaviour. Tolman's work gave birth to **expectancy** theory in the 1930s: we are motivated by conscious expectations of what will happen if we do specific things. (**V. H. Vroom** later tried to quantify these motivating forces, arguing in the 1960s that the strength of each motivating force equals the valence – or attractiveness – of the outcome, times the probability we assign to the outcome actually happening.)

Combining the behaviourist and cognitive approaches – but probably more in the former camp – was **Frederick Taylor**. His 1947 paper on *The Principles of Scientific Management* appealed to the large monolithic organisations which had emerged by that time. 'Take 15 particularly skilful men . . . study the precise sequence of elementary operations and use of implements . . . using a stopwatch, identify the quickest way to perform each element of work . . .'

However, the cognitive theorists were in the ascendant. By the late 1940s, **Douglas McGregor**'s exhortations to use **Theory Y**, rather than Theory X, were gaining followers. (Theory X: most people intrinsically dislike work; they therefore need to be controlled and coerced if they are to contribute towards the organisation's goals; most people want to be directed, have little ambition or wish for responsibility. Theory Y: work and mental effort are as natural as play; man will self-direct and self-control if committed to the organisation's objectives;

this commitment is a function of a variety of rewards associated with the work; in this environment the individual actually seeks certain responsibilities; most people have substantial potential to innovate; but this potential is largely untapped.)

Elton Mayo's work at the US **Hawthorne** plant in the 1930s was remembered: productivity is more affected by social pressures, group incentives and the fact that someone is making them feel important – and less a function of the length of coffee breaks, and other elements of Taylor's 'scientific management'.

The 1940s saw **Abraham Maslow**'s famous contribution on human needs (see below), and the 1960s and 1970s adopted **Frederick Herzberg**'s concepts. He reviewed the particularly high rates of staff turnover in certain corporations, coining the concept of 'job satisfaction' (the need to feed employees' loftier needs for achievement, recognition and 'self-actualisation'). He also helped to identify the existence of 'hygiene factors' – needs which have to be provided for at some base level, but which are unlikely to create greater efforts, even if the relevant rewards are delivered in higher doses. Herzberg believed **pay** to be only a hygiene factor in most cases.

Later decades reviewed the motivation of individuals more definitively from the viewpoint of the organisation's strategy and structure. Major contributions were **Alfred P. Sloan**'s decentralisation (articulated in 1963 after twenty-three years as the chief executive of the largest company in the world) and **Tom Peters**'s and **Bob Waterman**'s *In Search of Excellence*.

Psychologists have developed many frameworks and models during the last century. Exhibits 4 and 5 summarise two of the most widely useful ones.

Maslow asserted that we are all motivated to satisfy five essential needs, illustrated overleaf. These needs are related to each other in a **hierarchy**, with physical needs being the most potent. The most potent needs which are left unsatisfied tend to monopolise our immediate energy and efforts. But man is perpetually wanting: once a need is satisfied, the next higher need demands our attention. And the belief that a need will never be satisfied creates anxiety and dysfunctional behaviour.

Exhibit 4

MASLOW'S HIERARCHY OF NEEDS

Self-actualisation What we *can* and *must* be

Esteem . . . from self and others

Love . . . by – and for – others

Safety . . . Health, protection from violence and disaster

Physiology Food, drink, sleep, sex, sheer activity

Exhibit 5

DEFENCE MECHANISMS	
Defence	**Example**
Denial	'I have not been fired' (when really you have)
Repression	'Being with her was wonderful' (when it wasn't really)
Projection	'He hates me' (when really *you* hate *him*)
Displacement	'Why are you so difficult?' (when a third party is)
Sublimation	'I enjoy playing the violin' (but Rome is burning)
Regression	'Don't hurt me, I'm just a defenceless child' (from adult)
Rationalisation	'I had to hit you because there was a fly on your cheek'(!)
Reactive formation	'This is not a tiger, it's a cuddly cat' (but it really *is* a tiger)
Altruism	'I'll be a Samaritan' (so I can ignore my own problems)
Humour	'That cruel joke at my expense was very funny' (or was it?)

Anna and Sigmund Freud developed the notion of **defence mechanisms**, which we use to protect ourselves from painful anxieties. These anxieties can arise from external threats or from internal conflicts between impulses or beliefs. Long-term reliance on these mechanisms is considered unhealthy. You have been warned!

*   *   *

In our search for how to motivate ourselves and others, most of the approaches mentioned above have some nugget to offer us. Which theories we personally find most compelling and applicable will clearly be a function of our own individual psychology!

> *Two Principles in Human Nature reign:*
> *Self-Love to urge, and Reason to restrain.*

Alexander Pope (1688–1744)

Karl and Herman were both excellent lion-tamers, but they had different motivations. Karl delighted in exciting the crowd, while Herman mainly had a deep-seated desire not to get eaten.

Everyone has their own mixture of motivating factors

11. Personality Types

In which Alex is confronted by the rich tapestries of lives

'Thanks for that introduction to psychology,' said Alex, approaching Bea at the end of the lecture. 'Do you have time to answer a quick question? You've talked about people as if they're all the same. You did mention that different people might make different use of various defence mechanisms, but surely there is a more clear-cut system for defining different types of personality?'

'I'm afraid there's no magic formula. Why do you ask?'

Alex explained that he had become interested in motivation, and wondered whether – by knowing a person's 'type' – he could figure out more quickly how to motivate them.

'As with the analysis of almost any aspect of human life, the Ancient Greeks laid the basis in this area. Hippocrates thought that different people had different mixes of what he called "humours". Some people were more Melancholic, others more Phlegmatic, others Sanguine and others Choleric.

'This classification didn't help much in establishing how different types of people tend to interact with each other – and with the world – but it was, at least, a start.

'Jung, whom I mentioned in my talk, made the first real progress. His work coined the now-familiar terms "introvert" and "extrovert". Then he . . .'

Alex interrupted, 'Excuse me, but how does the introvert/extrovert distinction help us in daily life and in motivation, as opposed to in the clinic?'

'People whom we call "introvert" prefer to direct their energies "inwards" in some areas of their lives (not necessarily *all* areas). When compared with "extroverts", they prefer ideas and concepts over people and things; prefer concentration to interaction; often prefer reflection over action; they tend to think-do-think, rather than to do-think-do. Does that make sense?'

'I think so,' reflected Alex. Rob and Kate had sprung to mind. Rob had always worked with computers and mathematical models and seemed to prefer coming up with the absolutely correct answer before testing it in discussion with others. Kate, on the other hand, had always been involved in team sports and preferred to talk things through with others when solving problems. Rob always thought that Kate was unable to reach 'the answer' by herself, and Kate thought that Rob was interpersonally challenged – but perhaps they just differed in their preferred styles, rather than in their abilities.

'So how would this affect the ways in which introverts were motivated, when compared with extroverts?' pursued Alex.

'First,' replied Bea, 'in terms of *the subjects about which they would like to be motivated*. I think you can imagine the different types of challenge that each would prefer to tackle. Second, in terms of the *underlying motivating factors*, I don't know of any research which links the introvert/extrovert dimension to things such as the wish for money or wish for influence. Third, however, there are obviously differences in the *way in which you might help* these two different types of people to become motivated.'

'There are?' asked Alex.

'Yes. You asked during my lecture about the VICTORY cycle. You obviously know something about motivating people. Now, someone who prefers the introvert approach is probably going to be more keen to understand the VICTORY cycle as a concept first and then to apply it afterwards. Whereas an extrovert type would probably prefer to try out some simple tips on themselves or others and then see the whole theory afterwards.

'If you take another example of how people differ, the implications for motivation may be even clearer. Some people prefer to be highly organised, planned and regulated. Others prefer to be more flexible, spontaneous, and "go-with-the-flow". With the former, you would probably want to have an explicit plan for how they would motivate themselves. The latter type of person would probably tune out quite quickly if you tried that approach.'

Two people sprang to Alex's mind. His old boss was even more of a planner than Alex himself. It was impossible to excite him about acquiring a company unless you had a meeting with an agenda laid out clearly (and adhered to rigidly). Alex's wife Sarah, on the other hand, preferred a more flexible approach than Alex did – often exhorting Alex to be more spontaneous. It was much easier for her to become excited by the prospect of a last-minute vacation than by the prospect of comparing travel brochures months – or even weeks – before the holiday.

Bea continued, 'This topic of personality "types" is a large one. Give me your business card and I'll send you a brief summary of the frameworks which appear to be most useful. Some of them work better if you're trying to promote teamwork, others are better if you're trying to resolve conflicts. However, I know you'll find them worth bearing in mind.'*

Alex thanked Bea for answering his questions and joined the crowd at the bar. He couldn't help trying to tell the introverts from the extroverts and to distinguish the planning types from the spontaneous ones.

---

*Copies appear at the end of this chapter.

Defining Different Types of Personality

To motivate someone requires that we interact with them. This in turn means that we need to understand them – to know what type of personality they have.

Categorising anything can be dangerously simplistic or can be insightful and helpful. This is especially true when we attempt to categorise something as complex as a person.

All too often we brand people: 'dynamic', 'lazy', 'inspiring', 'thoughtful'. These simple descriptions rarely describe the essence of the person and rarely help us to interact with them, or to motivate them.

Over the millennia, there have emerged various frameworks for 'understanding' people's personalities. The opposite page sets out the more important approaches.

Caveat

Be careful when using personality profiles. They usually measure the way in which a person *prefers* to operate or interact with others. These profiles don't necessarily equate with the way in which the person actually behaves, or necessarily with their *ability* or *potential* to use or develop a specific style.

Taxonomies of Personality Types

1. **Meyers-Briggs Type Indicator** defines sixteen types of personality, based on where the person directs their energy (Extrovert vs Introvert), what they pay attention to (Sensing vs Intuition), how they make decisions (Thinking vs Feeling), and their orientation to the outside world (Judgement vs Perception). Appendix E provides further information.

	Sensing:		Intuition:	
	Thinking	Feeling	Feeling	Thinking
Introvert: Judgement Perception				
Extrovert: Perception Judgement				

2. **Herrmann Brain Dominance Indicator** maps, in a visually engaging way, the preferences for using the four quadrants of our brains.

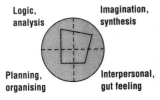

Logic, analysis — Imagination, synthesis — Planning, organising — Interpersonal, gut feeling

3. **Belbin's** approach focuses on team roles, with nine primary types: Shaper, Monitor evaluator, Team worker, Implementer, Completer, Specialist, Plant, Resource investigator, Co-ordinator.

4. **Hippocrates** (c.460–370 BC) was one of the first to analyse personality types, based on the individual's mix of the four 'humours'.

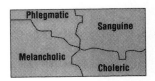

Phlegmatic — Sanguine — Melancholic — Choleric

'Are you kidding? I *like* it here!'

Cancel negative 'self-talk' and delusion

12. Fear of Success and Other Reasons Not to Be Motivated

In which Alex learns about mutiny and self-sabotage

Project Excalibur was now six weeks old. Despite a few early problems, it was now going well . . . worryingly well. In fact, it was in danger of becoming a major success.

The team had identified the types of customer complaint which had appeared most frequently, had discovered some of the production problems which had led to the product defects and had started to calculate the financial costs and benefits of taking corrective action.

Alex's job search was also proceeding well. He had talked with a few old friends and former colleagues and had even received a few unexpected calls from headhunters. Some of the jobs sounded exciting, though Alex thought that some of the roles might be too much for him.

The telephone rang. It was Bea. 'What a pleasant surprise,' responded Alex. 'Thanks again for that lecture on psychology last week. Very helpful.'

Bea asked whether Alex could spare a few minutes. She was in the building, having just finished a personal coaching session with one of her clients in the company. She appeared in Alex's office a few minutes later.

'I thought you might like some help. I guess the project's not going so well.'

'Why do you say that?' asked Alex, surprised.

'Well, I was upstairs in the canteen, and overheard a few people who I think are working with you – Project Excavator?'

'Excalibur,' corrected Alex.

'Exactly. Well, the team members didn't seem very positive when they were discussing the project with the others over lunch. They didn't give the impression that they were having much success.'

Alex explained that the project was going very well indeed; the progress was exceeding everyone's expectations. His look of surprise turned to one of puzzlement.

Bea thought for a minute. 'Perhaps they're developing a fear of success,' she mused out loud.

'Fear of *failure*, you mean.'

Bea reiterated that she meant a fear of *success* and proceeded to answer Alex's quizzical expression with a brief explanation.

'First, the fear of failure which you mentioned. You have to be rather careful when you use that expression, because it has two quite opposite meanings. One meaning is: "*I'm afraid of being a failure in life, so I had better drive myself to achieving excellence.*" This is a fear which activates and motivates (sometimes too much). The other meaning is: "*I'm afraid that I might fail if I try to accomplish this specific task, so I had better not attempt it in the first place.*" This is a fear which prevents people from taking initiatives. It potentially demotivates us.

'But fear of *success* is something different. It goes like this: "At the rate things are going, I am in danger of becoming successful. But I don't know if I'll be comfortable being successful, so I'd better slow down a bit. That way I won't have to go to the effort of adjusting to the success."'

Alex wriggled in his seat. Although Bea's statement sounded implausible, he thought he caught a glimpse of a few symptoms in himself. 'But why would people feel uncomfortable with success in some area of their life, or with success in life generally?' he asked.

'There are a million reasons,' she continued. 'How about: "*I don't deserve to succeed, because someone or some event has convinced me that I'm not worthy of success,"* or, *"If I'm successful, then I can only go downhill from there, and I don't like going downhill,"* or, *"If I am successful, it will be more difficult to keep up my reputation – I will be swept into a vortex."* Subconsciously, one of my clients was even saying, *"I don't want to succeed in improving my relationship with my husband because then there would be no excuse for him continuing to be unfaithful to me – there would be proof that he doesn't love me."'*

Alex was getting the message. But how did this relate to his team? Bea knew that they used to have the nickname of 'The Faded Five'. She suggested that they might be having difficulty in completely casting off their old, low-key, low-profile, comfortable identity.

'But how do you fix this kind of problem?' continued Alex.

'During the lecture I gave last week, you mentioned the VICTORY model. The antidote to "fear of success" is all in that model. You know the answer already. It's all about rewriting the scripts for those dialogues which we have with ourselves. Talk to the team. Find out how they're feeling. You might need to convince them that it's OK to be successful! Try a bit of "Out with the old, in with the new". After all, the New Year is only a month or so away.'

'I must admit that I'm a bit fearful, myself,' said Alex. 'I'm looking for a new job. There are some pretty interesting roles out there,' he continued, 'but I'm not quite sure I'm up to them.'

Bea looked at him askance. 'Fear of success, or just lack of confidence?' she asked mischievously.

'A bit of each?' he ventured. 'But how about you, do you ever experience fear of success?' he continued.

'Never,' Bea replied, '. . . well, sometimes,' she confessed with a smile.

Fear of Success and Fear of Failure

Fears are powerful urges which can drive us to perform amazing feats, yet which can also inhibit us from even *attempting* other goals. For example, the fear that we might 'fail in the game of life' can drive us to marshal our skills and to excel. But the fear that we might 'fail if we try to change ourselves' can inhibit us from even attempting the unfamiliar. If we are to motivate ourselves or others, we need to guard against the inhibiting power of fear.

The taste of inhibiting fear comes in two main flavours:

- **Fear of failure.** We are usually familiar with this taste. We are sometimes afraid to make a presentation before a large audience, to ski fast downhill, to take on new challenges. Our fear is that we will be criticised or ridiculed – by other people, or by ourselves – if we fail.

- **Fear of success.** This flavour is more subtle. More paradoxical. Often we don't realise that it's there. But deep down, people are often afraid of being *too* successful. Justified by self-talk such as, 'I'm just fine the way I am', we convince ourselves that we just don't deserve to succeed, or that the mantle of success will neither fit nor feel comfortable.

* * *

Confront your fears and become their benevolent slave-master! Seek – or give – encouragement. Refer again to Appendix D, page 126.

Fear of Success and Fear of Failure

Fear of Failure

'I had better not try, because if I fail then people will just think I'm stupid.'

'If I fail, then *I'll* think I'm stupid.'

'I tried it before and it didn't work.'

Fear of success

'I don't deserve to succeed (because something or someone has convinced me that I'm unworthy).'

'I don't want to succeed, because I'm comfortable with the way things are.'

'I don't want to succeed because I won't like the new lifestyle of success.'

'I don't want to succeed because people will stare at me, and I'll be forced to be "impressive".'

'If I'm successful, then people won't give me their sympathy any longer.'

'I might get addicted to succeeding and that will require even more effort, all the time.'

'It's so simple that there must be a trick.'

'It will only be downhill from there – nothing left to hope for.'

Andy was a sucker for new technology.

Carrots are more powerful than sticks

13. Destroying Motivation

In which serendipity helps Alex to a chance discovery

As he headed home for the weekend, Alex had only intended a quick visit to the second-hand bookshop. He was looking for a copy of *Build Your Own Garden Shed*, which he needed for his next attempt at home improvement.

But the bookshop provided Alex with too much temptation to browse. (As a browsing addict, for example, Alex had avoided any contact with the Internet. He knew that any adventure into cyberspace would result in him becoming 'missing, presumed dead'.)

His guard was down as he scanned the shelves . . . and his gaze alighted on a battle-worn copy of *Depersonalisation and Demotivation – Handbook of the Montevideo Secret Police.**

Intrigued, he skimmed the contents and the first few pages. The more he read, the more he winced and grimaced. Not only were the techniques cruel and grotesque, they were also rather too familiar to anyone who had spent time in large organisations . . .

As he added the book to his pile of imminent purchases, he thought back to several people with whom he had worked over the years: the best secretary he had ever had – who had resigned unexpectedly; the outstanding candidate whom he had tried to recruit to his department several years ago – who had inexplicably turned down the job offer; his classmates at business school – who had seemed to exclude him from all social activities for a few months. Could these events have had *anything* to do with whether or not other people found him motivating? Surely not!

He paid for the books and set off home.

---

*See the following pages.

EXCERPT

Depersonalisation and Demotivation

Techniques of the Montevideo Secret Police

CONTENTS

CHAPTER 3: BREAKING THE WILL

It is important to break irretrievably the will of the subject. This can be accomplished using the following five steps, which are explained in more detail on subsequent pages:

1. Shatter all visions and hopes of escape, release, provision of food, relief from pain, etc.
   - Disorientate (e.g. unpredictably change the prisoner's environment [location, layout of cell, timings of meals, etc.])
   - Punish (e.g. respond immediately and severely to any attempts to escape or to personalise his environment)

2. Grind down the confidence.
   - Degrade (e.g. enforce menial activities)
   - Punish (e.g. administer shocks when prisoner is unable to accomplish impossibly difficult tasks)
   - Depress (e.g. phase all confidence-destroying actions with consistently increasing severity)

3. Remove any scope for voluntary actions.
   - (Note: this is an important step, since the subject is in danger of building self-esteem from the successful accomplishment of even minor tasks which he has chosen to undertake)
   - See separate chapter

4. Bombard with negative messages.
   - Ridicule (especially in front of other people)
   - Lie (e.g. tell the subject that his health is becoming fatally poor)
   - Deprive of all sensory stimulation (see 'Solitary Confinement')

5. Systematically destroy the subject's image of himself.
   - Shock (e.g. show the subject photos, or other evidence, of his declining condition)
   - Deconstruct (e.g. use different strategies unpredictably for different aspects of prisoner – physical, emotional, spiritual, etc.)
   - Negative role model (e.g. show how others in the subject's position have been destroyed)

Only Sergeant Kanarec would ever know why he was wearing enormous clown's shoes on that fateful morning . . .

Don't get caught in chain reactions of negativity

14. The Domino Effect

In which Alex suffers knock-on consequences

It all started when he accidentally banged his thumb with the hammer. That was on Saturday morning, in the garden, as Alex was putting the finishing touches to the new shed. Inflamed by his inability to wield the hammer properly, Alex aimed a kick at the doorpost of the newly erected structure. The door frame caved in and the remainder of the shed followed quickly. 'I can't be very good at home improvements,' Alex concluded.

He slunk indoors. 'Hi, Uncle Alex.' It was his nephews Jack and David, on a surprise visit with their parents. The real purpose of the visit, it transpired, was to seek Alex's help with David's maths homework.

The required mathematical proof had confounded David, then dumbfounded his father, 'They give these questions to *fifteen*-year olds these days?' But it was all going to be OK because Uncle Alex knew everything about maths.

Needless to say, Alex was not successful in uploading his maths skills from an infrequently used part of his memory. 'I don't seem to be that good at maths any more,' apologised a crestfallen Alex to a disappointed David.

Things went from bad to worse when Alex had a row with Sarah the next evening. The argument started from insignificant beginnings, skirted dangerously close to the subject of the garden shed and ended with the conclusion that Alex was a Bad Husband.

As he drove to the office the next morning, his back stiff from sleeping in the unfamiliar guest bed, he catalogued his recently awarded honours: Bad Husband, Bad Mathematician and – most galling of all – Bad Home Improver. Erroneously consoling himself with the belief that bad things only ever came in threes, he failed to observe the impending and unavoidable cyclist. He was about to become an official Bad Driver, too.

Reversing the Domino Effect

Most of us are familiar with the domino effect. A feeling of failure or dissatisfaction at work can have knock-on effects at home, or vice versa. Include health, wealth and wisdom as potential ingredients and the potential for the domino effect increases exponentially.

Yet some people seem to remain upbeat, even if they are experiencing trauma in one aspect of their life. How come? As we keep ourselves and others motivated, there are two things we can do about – or with – the domino effect.

- **Keep different types of domino separate.** Metaphorically, you put separate groups of issues into separate boxes and deal with them separately. That way, the issues are less able to interfere with each other. Of course, there is a danger in using this strategy for long periods at a stretch: it may just be that all the different areas of your life are trying to give you the same important messages! By 'dividing and conquering', you may eventually repress an important message from yourself.

- **Run the domino effect in reverse.** If some area of your life is going well, why not try spreading the virus of confidence and motivation to other areas? You are probably the best person to figure out how to use this strategy on yourself.

* * *

While there are no easy antidotes to the domino effect, you can help build the motivation of yourself and others significantly just by unmasking it, and being aware of its existence.

How Good and Bad Feelings Influence Each Other

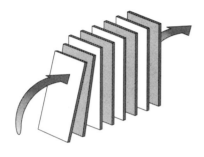

Normal domino effect: negative feelings regarding one area of life (white dominoes) can create negative feelings in other areas (shaded dominoes). The 'infection' normally operates through treating 'confidence' as an indivisible thing and by subconsciously re-scripting ourselves in a negative way.

Segregation: if you are having problems, try to separate the different types of domino to avoid 'infection'. Then you can focus your efforts on coping separately with each type of issue. Review Chapter 5 (Confidence) and Chapter 8 (Responding to Feedback).

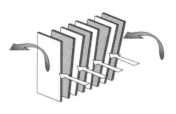

Reverse domino effect: if things are starting to go well, re-combine the dominoes, to reap maximum benefit.

Exercise

- Identify how prone you are to the domino effect and whether you ever manage to segregate your dominoes, or to run the process in reverse.

The whizz-kids upstairs may not have respected Carruthers's experience, but he did know where the power switch was . . .

Respect your elders . . . and your youngers

15. Baby Boom Meets Generation X

In which Alex has a theory, but cannot prove it

Alex arrived in his office stirred, but not seriously shaken. Fortunately, his road accident had not been serious, resulting in damage only to metal and not to man.

This was just as well, since he needed to resolve a growing conflict between Bill and Emma. They had made reasonable progress in the early part of Project Excalibur. As the team had discovered some of the production problems which had led to the customer complaints, Bill and Emma had followed up with the relevant production departments in the company. Their goal was to verify the hypotheses about what was going wrong and to persuade the production managers to fix the problems.

Although Alex had managed eventually to banish the team's 'fear of failure', progress was slowing. And they only had a few weeks in which to finish the project. In the plants which Bill was addressing, the production managers seemed to have agreed with the general concept of the project. But Bill was not managing to pin them down to agreeing specific improvements in their production processes.

By contrast, in Emma's departments, a few ideas of very high value had emerged. But no one knew whether there might be further opportunities and the production managers did not seem to understand the overall logic of the project.

It was as if Bill had used a 'top-down' approach, starting with the general issues, then moving (too slowly) to the specific ideas for improving the production processes. And it seemed that Emma had used the reverse approach, latching on to some very specific ideas, then moving (but not sufficiently far) towards the bigger picture.

Whatever the reason for the difference between their approaches, that difference was now creating a problem. As they started to summarise their results, Bill and Emma were becoming increasingly annoyed with each other. Bill wanted to summarise the results one way, Emma argued for a different form of summary. Bill wanted to build into the presentation more of the background context, Emma wanted to dive straight into the highest value ideas.

'Perhaps the difference in approach has something to do with their age difference,' thought Alex. 'After all, Emma is only twenty-five, while Bill is forty-five.'

*   *   *

He had a chat with them. As he went to see them in turn, he was struck by the differences in the layouts of their offices. Emma's Internet browser beckoned passing cybernauts; Bill's battered briefcase lay open on his desk. Emma's street-cred posters contrasted sharply with Bill's photos of his family. Emma's bookshelf sported titles such as *Click Your Way to Success – the Woman's Guide to Taking Control of the Internet*; they would not naturally have rubbed covers with Bill's well-thumbed *Ease Your Way to Retirement*.

Alex spent fifteen minutes with Emma, and a similar length of time with Bill. To make some fast progress in resolving the problem between them, he dared to hypothesise and simplify. 'Well,' he thought, 'age probably does play a part in what's going on here. Bill's longer experience in the corporate world has taught him the value of having all the appropriate players – such as the production managers – understand the background to the project. That way, he feels that there will be fewer hold-ups when the time comes to implement these ideas. On the other hand, Emma's youthful exuberance may encourage her to be more daring, and possibly to "go for" ideas and approaches which Bill (rightly or wrongly) might dismiss as impolitic.

'But is it really an issue of their *current ages*, or is it instead an issue of the *ages in which they were born and raised*?'

For example, Generation X (born in the 1970s) grew up in a world where opportunities were so many, varied and fleeting that they had to 'click to survive'. Not just click on laptop computers, but click on virtually everything.

Baby-boomers (born in the late 1940s and early 1950s) were products of a different adolescence. While they could catch up and learn the *skills* of clicking, few would probably want to change to adopting a thorough-going clicking *mindset*.

* * *

'I wish I'd thought about this earlier,' said Alex to himself. 'I would certainly have structured their responsibilities differently.

'I'm sure Emma would have been more motivated by a role richer in "clicks", and Bill by a role where he could have applied his experience more directly.

'But perhaps the current arrangement is not such a bad approach. Perhaps Emma will learn something from Bill, and – more importantly for Bill – perhaps he will learn something from her.'

Alex realised that he was speculating. He knew that age-ology was important, but he didn't have the answer. He doubted if anyone did.

Nevertheless, he confronted the issue openly and encouraged Emma and Bill to do likewise, with some success.

The Generation Gap – Abyss or Hairline Fracture

The 'generation gap' is an elusive gap. Some feel that substantial differences exist between people aged, for example, twenty-five and fifty. Others feel that the differences between individuals *within* a generation far exceed the general differences *between* generations. Still others believe the former, but claim the latter!

In some areas, such as in science, we rely significantly on experts. But when it comes to helping much older or much younger people to become more motivated, our beliefs are more likely to be conditioned by our *own* experiences when younger and older than by the views of others.

Nevertheless, society changes at an accelerating rate. It would be surprising indeed if some of these changes were not imprinted on the psyches of the children born of differing decades. And surprising also if the accumulation of an older person's experiences and responsibilities left no trace.

The facing page suggests some factors which you may want to bear in mind when helping older or younger people to become motivated.

Generation X and Baby Boomers

What sociologists say about Generation X . . .

Driving factors

- Negative world view (40 per cent divorced parents, parents' jobs restructured)
- Home-alone individualists (dual career parents, day care, cable TV, video games)
- Less loyal (political exposés, parents' jobs restructured)
- Questioning of authority (less present fathers, less military training, less church)
- More diverse (ethnic influxes and mixing)

Preferences for learning and living

- Feedback hungry
- Do-see-do (not learn then apply)
- Parallel processing (not step by step)
- Technoliterate, informationally opportunistic
- Fewer compromises in pursuit of fun
- Entrepreneurship and outcomes
- Clickable sound-bites, not lengthy speeches

When motivating *older* people, e.g. Baby Boomers, the following factors *may* assume greater importance.

- Fear of having failed, or not having accomplished enough
- Nervousness that technology will advance too rapidly for them to pick up
- Preference for patterns and logic, not just data points (however interesting)
- Preference for the concrete over the virtual or meta-virtual
- Concern for – or about – family

Exercise

- Talk about motivation with someone who is much older than you, then with someone much younger. Compare their perspectives.

Using 'Cheeseburger' as his smell of success, Noel went on to become the best – and the biggest – salesman in the history of the company . . .

Visualise your success – in all its dimensions

16. NLP – Neuro-Linguistic Programming

In which Alex picks up some very practical tips from a theory with a daunting name

Alex hoped that his third cup of coffee would wake him up, for he had an important job interview later that morning. The major competitor to Alex's company seemed very keen to hire him, although no one had yet had face-to-face discussions with him.

Before leaving for the meeting, however, he took stock of Project Excalibur. The team would be presenting its recommendations to the company's Executive Committee in ten days' time and the project was already starting to attract more interest than the team had envisaged. On the Committee's draft agenda, the project had already climbed from the foothills of last topic of the day to the more elevated position of being discussed 'mid-afternoon'.

Overall, the project seemed on track, but Alex was not so sure about his job search. The morning's interview was only the third which he'd managed to secure during the last six weeks. In addition, he felt very out of practice in the techniques of being interviewed.

At 10.30 he slunk nervously out of the building. He felt that he was simultaneously playing truant from school, breaking the laws which forbade competing companies from collusion, whilst also being insufficiently radical in the job options which he was exploring. He invoked all his skills of self-motivation in preparation. He formed an image of his imminent success in the meeting, boosted his confidence by recalling his previous mastery of far more difficult situations and prepared himself to take the plunge.

* * *

He returned two hours later, feeling that his interview performance had been reasonably strong. He wasn't sure, however, that he had really *engaged* with the man who had been sitting opposite him.

Turning into his office, he noticed Bea at the other end of the corridor. He beckoned her into his room.

'I've just been for a job interview,' he said, closing the door. 'Seemed to go well, but I'm not sure that the interviewer and I were quite on the same wavelength. Any thoughts on motivating someone to give you a job?'

Bea hesitated. She had a few ideas, but she thought that Alex might apply them poorly – in which case he might damage, rather than enhance, his performance. 'NLP,' she said eventually.

Alex always distrusted three letter acronyms: QED, PhD, TWA . . . 'And what's NLP?' he asked.

Again Bea hesitated. It was a big subject which did not fit easily into a five-minute discussion. 'OK, Alex, I'll give you a brief summary. But don't try using this stuff until you've learned more about it.

'NLP stands for Neuro-Linguistic Programming. It's a set of techniques which you could loosely describe as a toolkit for personal development and the achievement of excellence. As the name implies, it's based on "programming" yourself (i.e. your "neuro" circuitry) to act or react in certain ways, with a lot of attention paid to the use of "language" and other symbols and images.

'Its essential premise is that you can achieve just about anything if you can model and internalise the appropriate behaviour. In this context, "modelling" means a) seeing (and hearing, feeling, tasting, smelling) yourself in the act of achieving your goal, b) doing this through the use of your imagination, or from observing some expert in action, and c) staying alert to how well you're doing as you take steps to perform more strongly so that you can consciously fine-tune your approach. It's a bit like self-hypnosis, but it relies on both conscious *and* subconscious activity.'

Alex thought for a moment as he tried to digest this. 'But how could I use this to motivate someone else to offer me a job?' he asked, steering the conversation back to his prime objective.

'One part of NLP addresses the way in which we communicate. Research suggests that the impact of what we say is only 5 per cent related to the actual words we use! Forty-five per cent of the impact is driven by the tone, inflection and other characteristics of our voice and 50 per cent is driven by non-verbal things, such as the way we are moving and any actions which cause the other person to either trust or distrust us.'

'Oh,' piped up Alex, 'you mean all that stuff about power dressing and body language.'

'Not quite as simple as that, Alex, although those elements are important. You mentioned that you hadn't felt on the same wavelength as your interviewer. What made you think that?'

'Well, he had his arms crossed for much of the time, tended to look over my shoulder rather than at me, and seemed to go off at tangents in the discussion.'

'Those crossed arms of his . . .', Bea leaned forward, '. . . did you try to lean forward, or do anything else to open him up a bit?'

Alex found himself leaning forward toward Bea in response, suddenly realising that he was mirroring her action. With a wry smile, he also realised that – during the job interview – he had not even tried to get on to the same physical wavelength as the interviewer.

'More importantly,' Bea went on, 'you need to tune into the other person's way of thinking. Some people have a visual way of thinking ("I *see* what you're saying"), others are more auditory ("I *hear* what you want"), others are kinesthetic ("I *feel* I understand"). You have to use their imagery if you want to build rapport with someone.'

Alex was not entirely convinced, 'Sounds rather manipulative. Don't people see through this and then *distrust* you as a result?'

'Alex, everyone has intuition. If you're intending to be manipulative, then yes – people will recognise that. But you could say equally that you're doing the other person the courtesy of communicating with them in their own language – not just the verbal language, but the language of their tones, motions and emotions, too. As I said, there's much more to NLP than what I've just described.

'Find out some more about it – I guarantee it will help you with your interviews – and beyond.'

Neuro-Linguistic Programming (NLP)

NLP originated in the early 1970s. Since then it has developed into a practical toolkit for achieving excellence, successfully combining elements of linguistics, neurology and biology with research into the ways in which we communicate.

It involves 'programming' one's mind with images which are rich (and which are not necessarily linguistic). Its central tenets are as follows:

- We can achieve virtually *any* goal which we set for ourselves (e.g. speaking a new language, painting pictures, making presentations more clearly, solving problems more effectively).

- To develop towards our goal, we need to: a) generate an extremely rich image of what the goal actually is, and b) move towards that goal by consciously modelling ways which we or others have found helpful in the past . . .

- . . . but we will only advance rapidly if we stay alert to feedback from our environments and from ourselves, and modify accordingly our initiatives (and our mental models which relate to our mission).

- Critical to *all* of these steps is the need to engage *all* of our senses. We cannot communicate clearly with ourselves or with others if we limit ourselves to words alone.

*   *   *

NLP is widely regarded as the General Theory of Self-Development, and it's worth reading up on the subject.* This chapter is merely by way of an appetiser.

---

*See *Introducing NLP* in the Bibliography.

Fragments of NLP Unveiled

Neuro- How you use your senses to filter and process your experiences, and . . .

Linguistic- use language and symbols to create mental models, to build . . .

Programming new, ingrained, habits and modes of behaviour.

Selected NLP concepts (see Appendix F for descriptions)

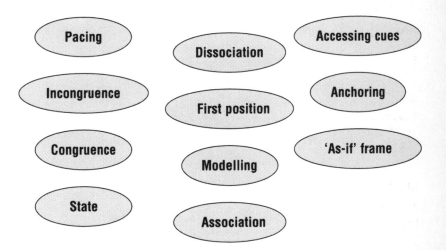

Pacing

Dissociation

Accessing cues

Incongruence

First position

Anchoring

Congruence

Modelling

'As-if' frame

State

Association

Exercise

- Read or skim a book on NLP. Watch a speaker whom you admire – note how he or she uses visual, auditory and/or kinesthetic images.

Unfortunately for Viv, the words 'neat landing' meant something *completely* different where the green, fat boy with the laser gun came from . . .

Deliver praise in a way which you know will be understood

17. Praise

In which Alex finds it difficult to be convincing

Alex was feeling reasonably confident about Project Excalibur's final presentation, which he would be delivering to the Board in just a few days' time.

The cost and revenue improvements were potentially much larger than the team had initially thought possible; to implement the proposals appeared to be a relatively straightforward matter; and, importantly, some of the company's larger customers were highly impressed with the approach which the team had taken.

But Alex was worried about Rob. He seemed incapable of accepting any praise. Despite Rob's slow start on the project, he had eventually delivered strong results – and Alex had had reason to praise his performance. No problems there.

What concerned Alex was that Rob would not be thinking radically enough about the positive career steps which he could now take. If he hadn't accepted the praise, then it was unlikely that he would be confident enough to apply for appropriately high-level positions via the company's internal placement market or with a different company.

* * *

Alex tried once again to get hold of Michael. He'd been trying to track him down for several weeks, but Michael just didn't seem to be returning his calls any longer. Alex wanted some advice on his own career plans, and was planning to add on a quick question about delivering praise to Rob.

Eventually, Alex had tapped into his voice-mail system and heard Michael's message: 'Sorry I haven't been in touch – there's a lot of going on at the moment.' The message continued with some general words of advice for Alex, and ended with a brief series of suggestions on how to deliver praise in a motivational manner.

* * *

Later that day, Alex met Rob.

'How are you doing, Rob?'

'Fine, thanks,' came the bland response.

'How about your next job – any thoughts yet?'

As Alex had expected, Rob did not seem to be setting his sights very high.

'Look Rob,' Alex felt like grabbing him and shaking some sense into him, 'you turned in some excellent results on this project. Shouldn't you now be aiming for some much bigger role?'

'But I'm not sure that I did *that* good a job . . . I mean, there were lots of other analyses I could have run.'

Alex hesitated. He was unsure whether, yet again, to address Rob's insecurities, or whether to focus just on making the praise stick. He chose the latter course. And used Michael's first suggestion: to **prove** that he meant the praise.

'Rob, regardless of the outcome of this presentation to the Board, I want you to know that you did a great job. *Whenever I need someone to extract real insights out of some complex data, you are the one I will call.*'

A few more minutes' discussion suggested to Alex that Rob still had not registered the praise. Alex moved to the second approach: to **explain** why he thought Rob's work had been so good. Despite appropriate illustrations, Alex felt that route was not working.

He was now determined to get his point across. He realised that he was overstepping the mark, but he went for it anyway: an overwhelming statement of the astronomical heights to which Rob would undoubtedly rise, based on the evidence of his strong performance. 'Rob, the only thing I can say is that you set yourself the vision of being a Merlin the Magician with the data. I just want to tell you that you are a god-damn WIZARD. One day you will probably own a software company, or perhaps you'll go back into the academic world. Either way, I'm sure you'll be famous for those skills of yours.'

Rob seemed to light up. His voice took on a stronger timbre. He looked Alex straight in the eye. 'Do you really think so?' he asked excitedly.

Alex, trapped by his own perseverance, owed it to Rob not to back down now. 'Absolutely,' he replied both with resolve and with fingers crossed.

* * *

Rob left, closing the door behind him. Alex, exhausted from his efforts, slumped more deeply into his seat. 'I wonder if I did the right thing?' he asked himself nervously. 'It didn't seem right to go so far.'

But a strange thing happened. Over the next few days (and perhaps for longer), Rob seemed much more positive and outgoing. Unknown to Alex, Rob had always wanted to start his own software firm and now he was taking the first exploratory steps in that direction.

Alex decided that – when it comes to providing praise – the end does justify the means . . . provided always that there is some real basis for saying that the job was well done.

Praise

You cannot motivate someone unless you are able to deliver praise for something which they have done (or for a skill which they have) *in an utterly convincing way*.

For some reason, most people expect that a statement like 'You did that really well' will be followed by '. . . but here's how to do it better'. For this and other reasons, many people will not accept the initial statement alone as genuine. At the very least, they'll feel that you're holding back some criticism. The table opposite suggests some approaches which you may want to adopt, to counteract this syndrome.

Of course, there are times – especially in the environment of work – where you may also want to suggest ways for the person to improve their performance.* Nevertheless, you should be careful to deliver enough *unadulterated* praise.

If you are trying to sustain your *own* motivation (rather than someone else's), then you will clearly need to find your own ways to convince yourself of your abilities.

---

*See *The Tao of Coaching*, Chapters 5 and 16.

Four Suggestions for Delivering Praise

Problem	Suggestion
Person cannot believe your positive comments.	*Prove* that you mean it: 'That presentation was so good that *I'd like you to make the next ones*', 'That photograph was excellent – *could you take some more for me, please?*'
Person does not really understand why you think they did a great job.	*Explain why* you think that what they did was good: 'That presentation was great *because* you . . .'; 'That photograph is excellent *because* . . .'
Person thinks they achieved a 'lucky' result.	*Suggest* that their performance is an indigenous trait: '*You are* a great presenter . . .'; '*You are* an excellent photographer . . .'
Person does not see their full potential.	*Express* their potential in a radical way: 'You are such a great presenter that you could become a TV news reader'; 'Taking photos like that, you could become famous.'

'Ooooo, this is gonna cost ya . . .'

Give yourself a stress check, before it's too late

18. Stress; Mind, Body and Spirit

In which Alex learns to distinguish stress from strain

Alex was nervous as he sat at the back of the boardroom, awaiting his turn to address the Executive Committee. The Excalibur team had prepared his slides, but he knew there were a few vulnerable areas within his presentation.

He envied the apparent ease with which the marketing director sauntered to the laptop which was linked to the projector.

'How come I'm so stressed while he's so relaxed?' wondered Alex. 'After all, we are in the same environment and we both have a lot of experience in making high-profile presentations.'

Then Alex remembered something from his engineering days: stress is the force which is exerted *on* an object, while strain is the way the force is transmitted *through* the object. Stress is external and strain is internal. So, technically speaking, both Alex and the marketing director were equally *stressed*, it's just that the stress was causing more *strain* within Alex.

As he doodled on his pad of paper, he wondered why his strain differed from that of the marketing director.

'Perhaps it's all in the mind. All this self-talk, all these "chattering monkeys" that meditation aims to quiet. I've done my experiments with meditation. It does seem to help. But I always feel that people who meditate regularly (sometimes for hours each day) have merely found a new activity to which to addict themselves. Instead of fostering the "non-attachment" which is its aim,

meditation can sometimes create a new form of attachment.'

Alex concluded that his mind was indeed OK (at least for the time being). He decided – and not for the first time in his life – to transcend the need to meditate! It was a great excuse.

'Perhaps it's my physical body that's responsible for the strain which I'm feeling. But I have a healthy diet. I suppose I don't exercise as much as I ought to, but I'm in pretty good shape for my age. I could still run a marathon if I really wanted to and if I put in enough training ... no, it's not a problem with the body. Perhaps I have had a few too many business dinners recently, but I don't think that they're to blame, either.'

He was about to move on to reviewing his spirit, as the third part of his mind-body-spirit trinity, but then he had another thought.

'We always think of diet and exercise when we think of "body". We don't so often think of reflexes and reactions – many of which have become so automated that they really are part of our physical bodies. How about the adrenal glands. That "Fight or Flight" stuff – is that part of "mind"? I think not – it's more part of "body".'

Even with this broader definition of 'body', Alex gave himself an acceptable pass mark on his brief self-examination. He did wonder, however, why most medical check-ups seem to pay so little attention to emotional reactions (focusing rather on purely physical knee-jerks). He would ask his doctor about this, next time he saw her.

'Then I suppose my strain must have something to do with my spirit. *What is "spirit", anyway?'* (He flipped open his palm-top computer and hit Tools, Thesaurus: *'Life, vitality, animation, dash, soul, essence. Hmmm ... not very helpful (as usual). Soul – that looks the most promising. Let's see what the Thesaurus has to say about that: ... life, vitality, animation, dash, spirit, essence.'*

Frustrated by the circularity built into his cut-price Thesaurus, he gave up his quest for his spirit.

With his presentation slot imminent, he concluded that it was very difficult to pin down a single cause of 'strain'. Perhaps that's why consulting psychologists always had such full schedules.

All one could do usefully was 1) stay aware of the distinction between stress and strain; 2) try not to expose oneself too often to situations fraught with excessive stress; and 3) hope that some general maintenance activities focused – even separately – on the mind, body and spirit would somehow combine to channel strain through the self in a way which was not too painful.

But Alex was brought sharply back to the reality of the boardroom by an argument which appeared to be brewing. It seemed that the marketing director had been ignoring a few questions from members of the Executive Committee . . . and not answering others fully enough! He had been so sure of himself that he had cruised though his presentation, not conceiving that his listeners might have something useful to contribute.

'Perhaps it's possible to be *too relaxed*, or *insufficiently stressed*,' Alex thought. 'We all need *some* adrenalin in our systems, to keep us on our toes. Without some stress, we'd be falling asleep – or failing to answer questions from the audience.'

Now it was Alex's turn to address the Committee. As he delivered his presentation, he was grateful for his adrenal glands after all. He ran through the proposals which Project Excalibur had generated, highlighting the potential to both increase profitability and simultaneously improve customer service. He was alert and responsive as he fielded the subsequent questions.

The Committee seemed impressed, but of course the Board of Directors would have to agree to the proposals in their meeting the following day.

'Stress'

Sometimes things go wrong. Then more things go wrong. Eventually, we start to feel overwhelmed. We start to feel stressed!

Or do we? Stress is a word often misused. But its misuse is subtle and subliminal, and therefore a particularly dangerous entry in our lexicon of self-talk.

Engineers, however, distinguish very clearly between *stress* and *strain*. Stress is the external force applied to a body; strain is the manner in which that force is transmitted through the body. While we may not always be able to control the external strains, we certainly can do something about the internal stresses.

OK. So what *can* we do to remain motivated, even when stressed?

- **Learn to distinguish** between stress and strain – put them into separate boxes and deal with them separately.

- **Recognise the *beneficial* effects of appropriate levels of strain** (and therefore of stress). Without these forces we would live uninteresting catatonic lives.

- **Identify your personal optimum zone** for stress and strain. Some of us need more stress than others, to operate effectively. Explore your personal stress boundaries; experiment with them actively – flex them up or down.

- **But** seek expert guidance if you feel completely overwhelmed.

* * *

Stresses and strains can either strengthen or weaken the linkages in the VICTORY cycle. Learn to play with them to your advantage (or help others to do so).

If you need further support in this area, any good bookshop will provide entire books (and seminars) to help you manage stress.

Stress *versus* Strain, and the Optimum Zone

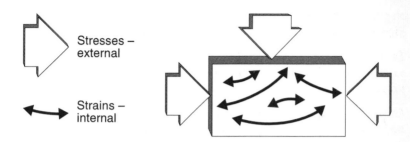

Stresses –
external

Strains –
internal

Different bodies react to stress in different ways. Some remain unchanged then suddenly snap. Others deform but do not break. It all depends on their 'degree of elasticity'.

With too little – or too much – stress for long periods of time, we tend to be less effective. We each have our own profiles and our own personal zones for the optimum amount of stress.

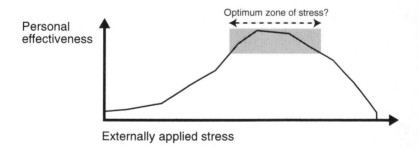

Personal
effectiveness

Optimum zone of stress?

Externally applied stress

Exercise

- Bring to mind some of your life. Describe your own 'degree of elasticity' in this area. Sketch your own profile of how your effectiveness varies with the amount of stress applied.

No one had spoken a word in the three days since Huxley had insisted on playing the 'rowing' game . . .

Don't leave your motivation skills back in the office

19. Motivation – Beyond the Workplace

In which Alex applies his recently acquired skills outside work

His presentation to the Executive Committee finished, Alex checked his watch, and set off for the Centre for the Homeless. Every year, as Christmas approached and the nights grew colder, Alex donated a few days of his time to this charity. At the organisation's headquarters, his skills in planning and logistics helped the right number of donated blankets, beds and gifts to arrive at the right places at the right times.

Despite his recent challenges at work – or perhaps as a break from them – he resolved to meet his commitment again this year.

* * *

New faces greeted him, and a few familiar ones. 'Hi, Alex – kept out of trouble since last Christmas?' It was Zak Daniels – perennially cheery, successfully entrepreneurial, and once again this year the temporary captain of the volunteer brigade.

'I've had a few ups and downs, but I'm feeling much more energised than I was a few months ago,' replied Alex.

'Glad to hear it.' Zak always brushed aside the past, focusing instead on the present and the future. 'We've got a few problems this year. Too many beds, not enough blankets, and I'm afraid that a few of the people working with you on the logistics are thinking of making this their last year as volunteers. Not sure why.'

Half of Alex groaned – this sounded like the saga of the Faded Five all over again. The other half of Alex remembered the comments of Jim, his boss, several months ago about how Alex was not a motivator. The latter half got the upper hand. He resolved to prove Jim wrong – Alex would take *any* group of people and motivate them.

Alex had to think fast. They had only three days to get the job done, and Alex had only fifteen minutes before the team arrived for their briefing. His natural inclination would have been to apply his excellent skills in organisation and planning, grooved through his years of engineering at university, production management in his first job, experiences at business school and strategic planning at his current company. But he paused. He would prove Jim and those other Directors wrong. He would focus on Vision and all the other elements of motivation, instead of planning and micro-management.

As the last few members of the logistics team arrived in the dilapidated room, he was still putting the finishing touches to his introductory remarks. To what visionary images could he appeal? What *very* simple plan of action might galvanise their efforts? What were the motivating factors which drew together these volunteers?

'*We are gathered together – now – here – on the eve of Christmas, in the presence of the homeless and needy. We will face tough challenges over the next three days, but we will surmount them. Not for money. Not for fame. Not for ourselves. But to be as owners of the inn, who gave shelter to those three needy travellers two thousand years ago . . .*

'*. . . and we're going to meet one final goal. We're going to have such a great time together in the next three days that we will look forward to joining together again, come next Christmas,*' he concluded.

Alex thought that the next few days might provide a less risky forum for practising his skills of motivation. He was in an environment where most of his team members did not know his usual analytical and controlling style. He could therefore be extreme in his experimentation, without worrying that others would be asking, 'What's happened to Alex? Why is he acting this way?'

Alex had consciously overcome his wish to 'control all the work himself'. He had built into his plan enough time to talk with each of the team members – checking and energising their own visions for the next three days' work, monitoring and boosting their levels of confidence, and observing and rescripting the ways in which they were responding to the apparent rate of progress.

* * *

The deadline approached. On the team's final afternoon, loaned lorries collected the beds, blankets and other items from a wide variety of depots. Some drivers went directly to the final drop-off points at centres for the homeless around the country. Other drivers dropped off at intermediate warehouses first, then took re-mixed loads out to the centres.

There were last-minute problems – some major, some minor. But as midnight struck to summon Christmas Eve, the team knew that their job had been well done.

As plastic cups and cheap plonk circulated, the team was in high spirits. Zak cornered Alex and shook him by the hand. 'Great job.'

'Thanks,' replied Alex.

'No . . .', continued Zak, again brushing aside the past in favour of the future, 'I mean I've got a great job to *offer* you. I'm about to announce a major takeover. Now I need some heavyweight character to run it. I've seen you at work over the last few years. And – I hope you don't mind – I've taken the liberty of checking out your credentials. So . . . are you interested?'

'Sounds like a great role. I suppose I'd need to know a bit more about the company.'

'Don't worry about that. I'm sure you know enough. Anyway, it's your motivational and management skills we're after.'

The clock struck one a.m., and Alex was saved from the need for an instant decision. He headed for home, promising to call Zak the next day. And he would . . .

Motivating Beyond the Workplace

Many of the examples which appear in this book illustrate applications of the **VICTORY** model in the setting of the workplace.

But the techniques and suggestions are applicable much more broadly. You probably don't aim to become a professional counsellor or motivator, but if you just 'spread a little motivation' then you can expect unexpected rewards.

- The chart opposite suggests a few areas in which you might want to apply your motivational skills.

- In reaching out in this way, there are a few points to bear in mind:

  - **Pay attention to the context.** At work, as a manager and leader of others, people expect you to motivate them (or at least they hope that you will). Although your friends and family may not share those same expectations as your colleagues, most probably share the same hope. Nevertheless, you should edge – or dive – into the motivation of others only after having thought explicitly about the context.

  - **Obviously** (but worthy of emphasis), you do not need to confine your uplifting efforts to someone who is 'down'. You might want to energise a person who is already motivated.

  - **Don't bite off more than you can chew.** Occasionally, people need help from a professionally trained psychologist – e.g. if they are clinically depressed. In these situations you should confine your efforts to motivating them to seek that professional help. Otherwise you risk making matters worse.

Motivating Beyond the Workplace

Areas in which to motivate

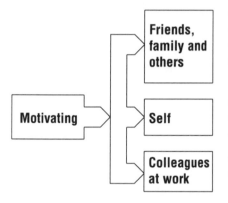

- Career: current, future
- Sport: learn, or improve, skill
- Voluntary work
- Life: in general, or specific event

- Health: exercise, diet
- Skill: language, other
- Habits: non-smoking, other

- Specific skills
- General attitude

Exercise
- Give yourself the luxury of applying your newly-honed skills, more broadly than you might originally have envisioned.

Sales were slow, and inside the store Hank was starting to wonder if he'd picked the right town in which to launch his new book.

Make motivation a habit

20. Mastery of Motivation

In which Alex reviews the steps along the way

The day before Christmas saw Alex back in the office for a morning's work, before the seasonal break. With any luck, he would hear whether the Board of Directors would adopt the recommendations which he and the team had presented, via the Executive Committee, several days earlier. After lunch with the team, he planned to set off home. He would call Zak to find out more about that informal offer of a job. Then he would make his decision, in the light of the one other offer which he had so far received – from the company's major competitor. But, over his first coffee of the day, he decided to review his past three months.

Project Excalibur: a success. Whatever the Board decided, Alex knew that the company would eventually implement the team's recommendations and would probably set up similar projects in Excalibur's wake.

The Faded Five: perhaps not an elite squad, but they'd certainly proved themselves – individually and collectively. Several managers from other parts of the company had been asking Alex about them. These managers had been impressed with what they'd seen, as the team members had worked with other members of their staffs to resolve the production issues. The team members had all been offered other roles in the company.

Alex himself: he gave himself 7½ out of 10. While he'd turned around the team's performance, he wasn't sure if he really was a master motivator (either of himself, or of other people).

He allowed himself a few minutes' reflection on what constituted mastery of the skill of *habitually* motivating oneself and others. Practising his skills of visualisation, he allowed an image of true mastery to emerge in his mind. It eventually appeared as an amalgam of Bea and Michael. So what did they do that worked so well and how had they arrived at this level of skill?

The most important characteristic of mastery seemed to be a combination of intuitiveness and instinctiveness. Both Bea and Michael had their tools, models and frameworks – many of which they had taught to Alex. But there was something else which made these two people true masters – they used their tools, models and frameworks with true instinct and intuitively applied the right ones to the situation at hand.

For example, Michael could explain the VICTORY cycle to you step by step if you wanted him to. But when he applied it – certainly in motivating others and probably when motivating himself – the cycle was no longer a series of steps in a circle. It was more as if the circle had shrunk to a dot. Or even a non-existent dot. Or even a non-existent dot which was part of all the other non-existent dots which had become a part of his self. Motivation had, for him, become an 'art-less art'.

But how had Michael and Bea achieved this level of innate ability? Alex showed his analytical side to take over for a minute. Their paths must have involved developing both *expertise*, through explicitly learning those tools and frameworks, and *experience*, through repeated practice and subconscious engraining. Alex concluded that the steps to becoming a master therefore seemed to be:

1. Seeker. You realise the importance and impact (to yourself and others) of the habits of motivation. You learn a few simple techniques and apply them in less demanding situations.

2. 'Learned Adept' and/or 'Practical Doer'. You learn more about the subject, and apply the new approaches in relatively familiar territory; then with increasing confidence, you apply your skills more broadly. This is the path of the 'learned adept', who probably prefers to 'think-do-think'.

But there is another way. You can take the few early lessons you have already learned and apply them directly in familiar territory; only when you need additional expertise and techniques do you reach out to acquire them. This is the path of the 'practical doer', who probably prefers to 'do-think-do'.

Of course, most people spend some time on each of these paths – the paths are not mutually exclusive.

3. Master. In the early stages of 'adept' or 'doer', things begin to seem unduly complicated, but with greater skill and practice motivation becomes habitually easier. As a master, people marvel at your generosity of spirit in helping others. They wonder how you sustain the energy when you give so much and so frequently and to so many people. Perhaps you can do this because it's all so easy – you do not really feel that you are giving anything at all!

In the words of a Zen saying:

Before Zen, mountains are mountains and streams are streams;
During Zen, mountains are not mountains and streams are not streams;
After Zen, mountains are mountains again, and streams are streams.

* * *

Alex looked up. It was Michael. He didn't look like a master any more. He looked crestfallen and apologetic. At least he was human after all.

'Don't tell me,' groaned Alex, 'the Board turned down the recommendations.'

'Oh no,' reassured Michael, 'they agreed them in two minutes flat.'

'So, why do you look so down?'

'I'm sorry, Alex . . . I'd wanted to tell you sooner, but I'm sure you realise that I had to keep things secret . . .'

Michael dropped on to Alex's desk a typed page, hot off the photocopier. Despite his insight into human nature, Michael was unable to explain the smile which spread – with dawning realisation – more and more widely across Alex's face as he read the headline of the press release:

BOARD AGREES SECRET TAKEOVER
OFFER FROM ZAK DANIELS

New management team to be announced next week

Mastering the Habit of Motivating Yourself and Others

Do yourself a favour – *addict* yourself to the positive habit of motivating both yourself and other people. The benefits will be more profound than I can describe here.

The least you owe yourself is to become a master in the art of motivating *yourself*. So what are the characteristics of a 'master', and how do we become one?

- **Masters.** The clearest hallmarks of a master are *intuition and instinctiveness*.

  Intuitively, the master knows exactly how much 'motivation' to pour into a given situation. Instinctively, he* uses the right approach: as soon as – or almost before – he feels lacking in confidence, there is a reflex reaction.

  Circuitry kicks in which has become 'hard-wired' through practice: perhaps it's the circuitry of the VICTORY model, perhaps some other reflex. He remotivates himself almost before he notices his own demotivation. Uncannily, he knows just how to do this for other people, too.

- **Pathways.** The facing page illustrates three possible pathways to mastery; Appendix G, page 131 provides tips on how to tread them. The paths build *expertise* cognitively, *and experience* through repeated practice in many arenas. We each choose our own path, based on the opportunities which we – or luck – provide.

*   *   *

Few of us become absolutely intuitive and instinctive masters. It is an unpalatable but unavoidable fact that the state of motivation is one which requires daily maintenance. It's more like having to brush your teeth every day than it is like 'suddenly' learning to ride a bike. But it's the best gift you can give.

---

*. . . or she

Becoming a Master Motivator

Mastery: intuition and instinctiveness, based on expertise and experience, built both cognitively and through practice.

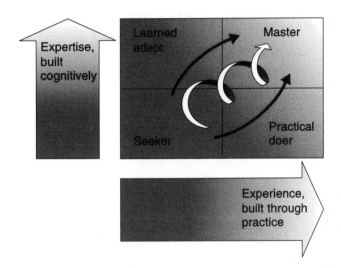

Exercise

- Decide on at least one person to whom you will pass on at least some of your skills in motivation, in the next three months.

Summary

- The skill, art, craft, and habit of motivating yourself and others is the hallmark of the excellent leader (and parent and friend). To motivate someone is to give them an invaluable and unforgettable gift. To motivate someone also requires that you, yourself, are motivated.

- It is possible to talk about and influence motivation in general terms, but it's best to start by focusing on a specific project or area of life.

- The VICTORY cycle is a simple, self-reinforcing model which helps most people. With an energising vision to create impetus, confidence is strong, efforts are redoubled, results impressive, feedback uplifting and confidence reinforced. You can start this cycle anywhere, but it's usually best to start with the compelling vision.
  - The **Vision** must engage all senses, and lead to practical plans. It illuminates all other parts of the cycle.
  - The **Impetus** to change needs to harness deep-seated urges.
  - Tend **Confidence** as a garden: seed it, feed it, weed it.
  - **Taking the plunge** can be pleasant, but is sometimes daunting; cultivate a voice to urge you at the moment of truth.
  - **Outcomes** should be planned, but not too much; plans are irrelevant, but planning is everything. Seek serendipity.
  - Effectively **Responding to feedback** requires that you script constructive self-talk, and monitor your system of beliefs.
  - **You** are the product of your motivations and resulting actions; use deep-seated motivations as well as the VICTORY cycle.

- Psychology is under-taught. Learn about the basics: defence mechanisms, personality types, fears of success and failure, the domino effect, NLP, stress versus strain.

- Most people need to do more of: delivering unadulterated and confidence-building praise (to themselves, and to others); speaking to the heart, not just to the mind; using simple one-page plans to make early progress; actively monitoring their self-talk and beliefs.

Finally, be natural and adapt to the needs of the person whom you are motivating. If you 'try too hard' and apply any techniques too rigidly you run the risk of appearing insincere and being ineffective.

Appendices

Appendix A
How to Use This Guide Effectively

You cannot become more skilled in motivating anyone merely by reading a book. Manageable chunks of practice are normally the key to success.

Therefore, you might want to adopt the following approach:

1. Complete a quick self-appraisal (Appendix B, page 123). This will help you to focus your practice, particularly if you ask others who know you to fill in a copy based on their impressions of you.

2. Pick a topic to practise this week – perhaps it's 'developing a vision', perhaps it's 'interpreting feedback'. Practise other topics when they appear most relevant and valuable to you.

3. Elicit feedback on your own progress in becoming a motivator of others. If you have a phenomenal success in working with someone, your feedback will come without you needing to request it. But usually – even if you are having a positive impact – you will need to ask how well you are doing, since most people will assume that motivators do not themselves need encouragement!

Appendix B
How Much Do You Motivate Yourself and Others?*

	Self			Others			Act	
	O	S	R	O	S	R	P	C
Vision								
Develop a compelling image – appealing to multiple senses – of what to be/do (for yourself or others)								3
Translate image into one-page plan (or support others in their planning)								3
Confidence								
Seek energising feedback from others; reward yourself (or others) tangibly								5
Know the specific factors which tend to enhance your confidence (or others')								5
Taking the plunge								
Avoid procrastination (or help others to do so)								6
Muster support from others – or from your inner resources – when on the brink of daunting action (or help others gain support)								6
Outcomes and obstacles								
Establish specific goals, which link to your vision in a simple and flexible way and which involve the pacing of manageable steps (or help others to do this)								7
Create serendipity for yourself and others								7
Responding to feedback								
Seek feedback, accepting credit for praise and using apparently negative feedback constructively (or help others to do so)								8
Monitor 'your self-talk', and rescript it if necessary (or help others to do so)								8

*Check (✔) your answers above (O = Often, S = Sometimes, R = Rarely), regarding how you motivate yourself and others . . . after that, decide where you will focus your efforts – ✔ P = Priority. (C = Chapter of particular relevance.)

Appendix C
Developing a Vision

You are the only person who can paint a convincing vision for you, though friends can help you.

- **Recall** the reason why you are reading this book. In what aspect of your life did you want to become more motivated? _____

- **Log** half an hour in your diary now, for an appointment with your-self to complete the facing page.

- During your appointment with yourself, **map** out your own vision for yourself; use the suggestions below if they help.

- **Congratulate** yourself on what you have achieved and schedule a further appointment with yourself if you would find it helpful. Review the thoughts which your friends had mapped out for you. Were you radical enough in painting your vision?

Become adept enough at this to help other people develop their visions. Ask others to help you develop yours.

Suggestions for your vision session

>> Ensure you are in a calm moment and place. Close your eyes, and dream of what success would look like.

>> Use all your senses to flesh out your picture - sight, smell, touch, taste, hearing and your sixth sense. Use metaphors.

>> Daydream more! What would be the title of your autobiography?

>> When ready, capture your impressions on the page facing this one - use drawing(s), colours, words; stick things to the page: whatever best helps you to capture the vision.

>> Jot down any ideas about actions, things or people which could help you on the way to fulfilling your vision.

Appendix D

Examining Self-Talk and Beliefs

'Interior dialogue' and our broader beliefs about how life *should* be often affect our level of motivation – positively or negatively.

The following suggestions may help. They are merely examples – no list could be exhaustive. So try to pick up the habit of developing your own, tailor-made, suggestions when you or others notice that you are being negative.

Problem	Suggestion
Self-talk – unhealthy habits (see Chapter 8)	
Generalising, irrationalising and transposing.	Actively monitor your comments about yourself (if you can!); convince a friend to help you do this.
Beliefs which are irrational (see Chapter 8)	
'I've *either* got to do A *or* do B.'	In addition to considering option C, establish how you can do *both* A *and* B – it's normally possible.
'People *should* treat me with respect – if they don't, then I must in some way be sub-standard/I'll have to attack them/etc.'	Remember that there are few universal truths in the way that people behave; solve your problem more effectively by starting with, 'I prefer people to treat me with respect, so . . .'
Self-talk – fear of success (see Chapter 12):	
'I don't deserve to succeed, because I'm convinced that I'm unworthy.'	Start with small steps if you must – surely there's *something* at which you deserve to succeed?
'If I'm successful, then people won't give me their sympathy any more.'	Consider that they may not give you their sympathy for much longer if you don't take some steps to help yourself.

Problem	Suggestion
(Self-talk – fear of success *cont.*)	
'People will stare at me, and I'll be forced to be "impressive".'	Review whether people are already staring at you, wondering why you are not more motivated.
'If I become more motivated, I will be drawn into a vortex of having to maintain an ever-higher reputation – that will be tiring.'	Assess whether you might actually be draining *more* energy to cope with your current state of *de-motivation*.

Appendix E

Elements of the Myers-Briggs Type Indicator (MBTI)

By analysing the answers to a number of 'trade-off' questions, the MBTI indicates a person's preferred approach to life, along four dimensions:

1. Energising (direction of energy)

Extrovert (E)	Introvert (I)
External	Internal
Outside thrust	Inside pull
Blurt it out	Keep it in
Breadth	Depth
People, things	Ideas, thought
Interaction	Concentration
Action	Reflection
Do-think-do	Think-do-think

2. Attending (perception)

Sensing (S)	Intuition (N)
The five senses	Sixth sense
What is real	What could be
Practical	Theoretical
Present	Future
Facts	Insights
Existing skills	New skills
Utility	Novelty
Step by step	Leap around

3. Deciding (trade-offs)

Thinking (T)	Feeling (F)
Head	Heart
Logic system	Value system
Objective	Subjective
Justice	Mercy
Critique	Compliment
Principles	Harmony
Reason	Empathy
Firm but fair	Compassion

4. Living (orientation to the outside world)

Judgement (J)	Perception (P)
Planful	Spontaneous
Regulate	Flow
Control	Adapt
Settled	Tentative
Run one's life	Let life happen
Set goals	Get data
Decisive	Open
Organised	Flexible

Appendix F
Selected Concepts from NLP

Concept	Description
Accessing cues	Using the body (breathing, posture, gesture, eye movements) to trigger a state (see below), or to access someone else's state.
Anchoring	Implanting a link between a stimulus and a response (e.g., a specific tune . . . which makes you happy; specific clothes . . . which make you confident).
'As-if' frame/ Future pace	Imagining that some event has happened, to solve problems and guarantee success (e.g., imagining the listeners as you rehearse a speech, to anticipate their responses).
Association/ dissociation	Being fully immersed in a thought or feeling/ observing yourself from a distance; used, for example, to ingrain new behaviours or to 'learn how you learn'.
First position (and second and third positions)	Being completely in touch with all dimensions yourself, as you experience or model (see below) an action. Second position: experiencing something from the 'receiver's' point of view. Third position: observing as if from a distance.
Congruence/ Incongruence	Having inner feelings and outer expressions which are consistent/inconsistent (e.g., smiling/frowning as you say 'this is easy').
Modelling	Analysing how someone accomplishes a goal, so that someone else can understand or copy the process. The basis for accelerated learning.

Concept	Description
Pacing	Gaining rapport with someone, and maintaining it over a period of time, by mirroring or matching them. You can pace beliefs and ideas as well as behaviour.
State (resourceful/ unresourceful) depression).	Experiencing a complete set of consistent feelings (e.g., the resourceful state of 'confidence', or the unresourceful state of

Appendix G
Tips for Mastering Motivation

Building expertise	Your plans?

- Identify which one or two techniques of motivation appeal to you.
- Observe and reflect as you apply them – amend them to fit your own style.
- Aim to adopt their use as second nature for yourself or others. For example, if you feel demotivated, then your VICTORY circuitry should 'cut in' automatically.

Building expertise	Your plans?

- Start by practising your skills in a situation where you feel comfortable. You may want to start by working on your own motivation rather than on someone else's.
- 'Edge out' into situations which appear to be more demanding – whether they relate to you or to someone else.
- Tailor the amount of motivation which you 'pour into' your interactions – it's not necessarily 'all or nothing'.

Bibliography

MOTIVATION

Attar, F	*The Conference of the Birds* (condensed version in *Tales from the Land of the Sufis* by M Bayat and M A Jamnia)	Shambhala Publications Inc, Boston, Massachusetts, 1994

In search of their leader, the thirty birds cross the Valleys of Quest, Love, Gnosis, Detachment and Unity, and then the Deserts of Astonishment and Annihilation. Eventually they discover . . .

Chopra, D	*The Seven Spiritual Laws of Success - a Practical Guide to the Fulfilment of Your Dreams*	Bantam Press, London, 1996

A Virtual Reality tool-kit for the 21st-century spiritual traveller.

Dante	*Divina Commedia*	Penguin Books, London, 1984

Illustrates how the journey to motivation and self-actualisation needs the guidance of both Reason and Faith, in the guises of Virgil and Beatrice.

Landsberg, M	*The Tao of Coaching - Boost Your Effectiveness at Work by Inspiring and Developing Those Around You*	HarperCollins *Publishers*, London, 1996

Tools and techniques to help you coach others and so become more effective yourself. In the same format as the book you are now reading.

Robbins, A	*Unlimited Power - the New Science of Personal Achievement*	Simon & Schuster Ltd, London, 1988

Techniques to reprogramme yourself, and to remake your world. Key words: syntax of success, confidence, emotional freedom, structure of beliefs.

Various	**(Auto)biographies**

Read a biography of a person who intrigues you; observe how they remained motivated.

PSYCHOLOGY

| Berne, E | *A Layman's Guide to Psychiatry and Psychoanalysis* | Penguin Books, London, 1968 |

A clearly written outline for the general reader. How the mind works when it develops normally; what can go wrong and why; what treatments are available for mental illness.

| Berne, E | *Games People Play* | Penguin Books, London, 1968 |

A brilliant, amusing and clear catalogue of the psychological theatricals that human beings play over and over again. A classic.

| Brizer, D | *Psychiatry for Beginners* | Writers and Readers Publishers, Inc., New York, 1993 |

A light-hearted – yet insightful – review of psychiatry and psychology. Illustrated with caricature-inspired art.

| Ellis, A | *Better, Deeper and More Enduring Brief Therapy: the Rational Emotive Behavior Therapy Approach* | Brunner Mazel, Inc., New York, 1995 |

A succinct and accessible guide to a very practical school of cognitive psychology.

| Keirsey, D & Bates, M | *Please Understand Me: Character and Temperament Types* | Prometheus Nemesis Book Company, Del Mar, California, 1984 |

Introduction to the Meyers-Briggs framework of personality types.

| O'Connor, J & Seymour, J | *Introducing Neuro-Linguistic Programming* | The Aquarian Press, London, 1993 |

The fundamental principles and tools of NLP – presented in an accessible and engaging format.

| Pope, A | *An Essay on Man* (in *Pope – Poetical Works*) | Oxford University Press, Oxford, 1966 |

Psychologist and poet intertwined,
Pope bared the soul, the passions, and the mind.

MANAGEMENT

Adair, J   *Effective Motivation*   Pan Books, London, 1996

A practical guide to motivation in the business setting.

Dunne, P   *Running Board Meetings:*   Kogan Page, London, 1997
                Tips and Techniques for
                Getting the Best from Them

Includes help on motivating top managers in the crucial setting of the Board Meeting.

Herzberg, F   *One More Time: How Do*   Harvard Business Review,
                You Motivate Employees?   (Jan–Feb 1968), Harvard
                Business School Press, 1968

Established the then revolutionary idea that motivating factors are distinct from 'hygiene' factors.

Kelly, K   *Out of Control*   Fourth Estate Ltd, London,
                1994

Evolution, coevolution and why attempts to control anything tightly are doomed to failure.

Maslow, A H   *A Theory of Human*   Psychological Review #50
                Motivation   (1943): 370–96; American
                Psychological Press, 1943

This paper sets out Maslow's thoughts on his famous hierarchy of needs; still applicable and widely-quoted.

Strage, H M   *Milestones in Management –*   Blackwell Publishers,
(editor)   *an Essential Reader*   Oxford, 1992

A unique collection of the original seminal articles which have advanced management thinking. Includes seven articles on leadership – including works by Maslow, Drucker and Herzberg.

GENERAL

Herrigel, E   *Zen and the Art of Archery*   Arkana, London, 1985

A great illustration of the master's instinctiveness-in-action.

Herrmann, N   *The Creative Brain*   Brain Books, North Carolina,
                1989

Extends the notion of left- and right-brain thinking. Illustrates applications to creativity, character and careers.

| Kozubska, J | *The 7 Keys of Charisma* | Kogan Page, London, 1997 |

Concepts and anecdotes that help to demystify the elusive notion of charisma.

| Scott Peck, M | *The Road Less Travelled* | Arrow, London, 1978 |

How to confront and address the problems of life.

Glossary

Baby boomers – Born of the late 1940s and early 1950s. (See Chapter 15.)

Behaviourism – Pavlov, Skinner and others' views that the person is an 'operant', the behaviour of which can be conditioned. They placed less explicit emphasis on the roles of motivation and of the subconscious.

Belbin Team Roles – A way of characterising a person's preferred role (particularly in teams).

Beliefs – Our model (implicit, and explicit) of how the world is, or how we would like it to be. When we experience adverse events, rational beliefs (prefer . . . hope that . . . wish to . . .) lead to healthy emotions and constructive action. Irrational beliefs lead to unhealthy emotions and destructive action. (See Chapter 8.)

Confidence – A state of faith in your ability to take initiatives towards a goal. (See *Feel*, *Seed*, *VICTORY*, *Weed*, and Chapter 5).

Defence mechanisms – Strategies which we use unconsciously to protect ourselves from painful anxieties. Short-term use of some mechanisms is considered healthy; long-term reliance is not. (See Chapter 10.)

Ego – One of three parts into which Freud's model divides the psyche. The *Id* represents instinctive urges, and operates on the Pleasure Principle; the *Ego* 'manages' our actions, and operates on the Reality Principle; the *Superego* represents our model of what 'correct' behaviour is and tries to interrupt 'inappropriate' actions. (See Chapter 10.)

Failure, fear of – Confusingly, the term *fear of failure* is often used in two distinct, and almost opposite, ways: a) a fear of **becoming a failure in life** (this urges us to take action to become successful), and b) a fear that we **might fail if we take a specific initiative** (this inhibits us from 'having a go'). (See Chapter 12.)

Feel (confidence) – Step 2 of building *Confidence*. Cultivating confidence by actively obtaining (or providing) reinforcement – e.g. from praise, self-acknowledgement, or mind-body-spirit connections.

Generation X – Born of the 1970s. Technophiles, clickers and parallel processors. (See Chapter 15.)

Herrmann Brain Dominance Indicator – A way of characterising a person's pre-ferred use of left- and right-brain (and upper- and lower-brain).

Humanism – Schools of therapy, developed by Rogers and others, which treat client's problems empathetically and holistically. Includes Gestalt Therapy and Transactional Analysis.

Id – See *Ego*.

Leadership – Creating a sense of mission based on: novel, visionary, yet practical ideas; inspiring others to join the mission and the team; monitoring and sus-taining the team's energy and the project's momentum.

Mastery (of motivation) – The state of habitually, instinctively and intuitively keep-ing oneself and others motivated.

Meyers-Briggs Type Indicator – A way of characterising a person's preferred per-sonality type. Has its origins in Jung's view of the psyche. It is widely used in the business environment.

NLP – Neuro-Linguistic Programming. (See Chapter 16 and Appendix F.)

Outcomes – Intermediate results – or 'stepping stones' on the path to achieving your goal. (See *VICTORY*, and Chapter 7.)

Regression – Falling back on coping mechanisms which worked at some previous stage of your life (sometimes childhood). Normally employed when stress is high. By implication, an unhealthy reaction.

Responding to feedback – The way in which we react to information about our progress towards our goals. Our reactions depend not only on the *Outcomes* we achieve, but also on the way in which our *Beliefs* and *Self-talk* filter and affect feedback. (See *VICTORY* and Chapter 8.)

Seed (confidence) – Step 1 of building *Confidence*. Using *Vision*, *Self-talk* and *Beliefs* to 'kick-start' confidence. (See *Feed* and *Weed*).

Self-talk – Messages – both conscious and sub-conscious – which we send to our-selves. These can be rescripted if they are undermining.

Serendipity – The art of generating positive, useful results from chance happen-ings.

Strain – Strains are externally applied forces – to be distinguished from *stresses*, which are our reactions to those forces. (See Chapter 18.)

Stress – See *Strain*.

Success, fear of – A feeling that inhibits us from taking initiative. For example, 'I'd better not try too hard, because I was not cut out to be successful – success would make me feel uncomfortable.' (See Chapter 12.)

Super-ego – See *Ego*.

Taking the plunge – Committing to take action towards a goal. *Self-talk* can help you if you are hesitating on the brink of taking a daunting initiative. (See *VICTORY* and Chapter 6.)

VICTORY – A powerful technique for helping yourself, or others, to become motivated. A virtuous cycle of *Vision, Confidence, Taking the plunge, Outcomes, Responding to feedback,* and *You.*

Vision – A rich and compelling image of what you want to be or do, which engages as many senses as possible. Both triggers and sustains the *VICTORY* cycle. (See *VICTORY* and Chapter 3.)

Weed (confidence) – Step 3 of building *Confidence*. Monitoring *Self-talk, Beliefs* and feedback to ensure that they sustain – rather than undermine – confidence.

Acknowledgements

The world of coaching and motivation is peopled by an unusually broad range of characters, a rich mixture of whom were generous enough to help produce this book. I thank them all greatly.

Ben Cannon (Worldwide Director of Training and Development at Goldman Sachs) somehow found enough time to provide several hours (and six pages) of comments. He should have written this book himself, but was too busy. Lucinda McNeile and her team at HarperCollins kept me motivated and grammatical. David Godwin, my maverick agent, sustained my confidence (and my discipline).

Nine other people - all distinguished professionals in the field of coaching and personal alchemy - were kind enough to share with me their insights: Susan Bloch, Peter Burditt, Heather Dawson, Graeme Delors-McNaught, Bob Garratt, Tom Lauda, Ruth Tait, David Westcott and Michael Worrall.

My parents, my sister, and several of my motivational friends also gave frank feedback and scintillating suggestions: Giambattista Aleotti, Charles Alexander, Costa Diamontopoulos, Kate Fleming, Petros Kalkanis, David Lieber, Stephen Powell, Dr Penelope Timpanidis and, especially, Eva Indra.

The direct and indirect impact of former colleagues and current friends at McKinsey & Company cannot go unmentioned. I particularly thank Partha Bose, Ian Davis and Norman Sanson.

Finally, I would like to give praise for his cartoons to my collaborator, conspirator and friend HIGGINS. In the pervasive game of tick-tack-toe he has proven again - as in *The Tao of Coaching* - that:

> though the pen is mightier than the sword,
> yet the brush is mightier than the pen.

Index